Case Studies on Diversity and Social Justice Education

Case Studies on Diversity and Social Justice Education offers pre- and in-service educators an opportunity to analyze and reflect upon a variety of realistic case studies related to educational equity and social justice. The accessibly written cases allow educators to practice the process of considering a range of contextual factors, checking their own biases, and making immediate- and longer-term decisions about how to create and sustain equitable learning environments for all students. This revised edition includes ten new cases to offer greater coverage of elementary education, as well as topics such as body-shaming, Black Lives Matter, and transgender oppression. Existing cases have been updated to reflect new societal contexts and streamlined for ease-of-use.

The book begins with a seven-point process for examining case studies. Largely lacking from existing case study collections, this framework guides readers through the process of identifying, examining, reflecting on, and taking concrete steps to resolve challenges related to diversity and equity in schools. The cases themselves present everyday examples of the ways in which racism, sexism, homophobia and heterosexism, class inequities, language bias, religious-based oppression, and other equity and diversity concerns affect students, teachers, families, and other members of our school communities. They involve classroom issues that are relevant to all grade levels and content areas, allowing significant flexibility in how and with whom they are used. Although organized topically, the intersections of these issues are stressed throughout the cases, reflecting the complexities of real-life scenarios. All cases conclude with a series of questions to guide discussion and a section of facilitator notes, called "Points for Consideration." This unique feature provides valuable insight for understanding the complexities of each case.

Paul C. Gorski is Associate Professor of Integrative Studies at George Mason University and the founder of EdChange and the Equity Literacy Institute.

Seema G. Pothini is a former classroom teacher, cultural integration specialist, and teacher trainer who now serves as an equity and diversity consultant.

Case Studies on Diversity and Social Justice Education

2nd Edition

Paul C. Gorski and Seema G. Pothini

Routledge
Taylor & Francis Group

NEW YORK AND LONDON

Second edition published 2018
by Routledge
711 Third Avenue, New York, NY 10017

and by Routledge
2 Park Square, Milton Park, Abingdon, Oxon, OX14 4RN

Routledge is an imprint of the Taylor & Francis Group, an informa business

© 2018 Taylor & Francis

First edition published by Routledge 2014

Library of Congress Cataloging-in-Publication Data
A catalog record for this book has been requested

ISBN: 978-0-8153-7498-5 (hbk)
ISBN: 978-0-8153-7500-5 (pbk)
ISBN: 978-1-351-14252-6 (ebk)

Typeset in Adobe Caslon Pro
by Swales & Willis Ltd, Exeter, Devon, UK
Printed in Canada

Dedication

Paul: For the Social Justice students at George Mason University. Thank you for the ways you've pushed me to grow.

Seema: For Kunda and Gurupad, whose strength and sacrifices I will always treasure. For Meena, Shrey, and Venu for being so incredibly loving, supportive, and patient with all my endeavors. And for the students and families I've worked with as an educator: your experiences continue to fuel my passion to ensure equity in our schools.

Contents

Directory of Cases by Topic

Curriculum and Pedagogy

Discipline, Engagement, and Classroom "Management"

School and Classroom Policy and Practice

School Culture

Programs

Parent and Community Engagement and Relations

Bias and Bullying

1

INTRODUCTION

"These people should learn English or we'll send them back to where they came from," Mayor Barton exclaimed to enthusiastic applause during his election victory speech. During a fiercely contested campaign, Mayor Barton relied on stoking racism and xenophobia in Dovetown to rally his base. The suburban town, which until recently had been predominantly white, was attracting growing numbers of Somali and Central American immigrants looking for work in its growing service industries. Although many people in Dovetown welcomed the diversity, others were not so welcoming.

Over the next couple weeks Ms. Samaya, a science teacher at South Dovetown School, noticed more and more sentiments mirroring Mayor Barton's statement surfacing, not only around the community, but in the school. She noticed the significant increase in racial and ethnic bias incidents targeting not only Somali and Central American students, but all students of color. Then, one night during an evening newscast when a reporter was interviewing local residents about the aftermath of the election, she watched as William, one of her neighbors, said he missed the "good old days" when everybody in the town knew one another and nobody had to worry much about "outsiders." Citing one of Mayor Barton's campaign claims despite it having been debunked by the town's sheriff, William stared into the camera and said, "Those people bring crime into my town and take our jobs." A group of people standing behind William clapped and cheered.

Ms. Samaya was concerned for her students. She was concerned for those who were part of the communities targeted by the racism and xenophobia displayed so brazenly by William and shared by many other adults in town. And she was worried for the children who were being socialized by parents to adopt William's views. As a child of immigrants, Ms. Samaya was fully aware these views had always existed to some extent in the town. But Mayor Barton's election had given people permission to share them publicly and many were doing so.

Although many teachers at South Dovetown were chatting informally about the election and the increase in bias incidents, Ms. Samaya was frustrated that the principal, Mr. Smith, had not addressed the issue with the full staff. She felt anxious about the upcoming staff meeting, hoping he would mention it.

Nothing is simple when it comes to diversity and social justice. Perhaps we can all agree that each student *ought to* have access to equitable educational opportunity—that a student's (or, for that matter, a teacher's or administrator's) racial identity, ethnicity, socioeconomic status, sexual orientation, gender identity, or home language should not determine her level of access to educational opportunity or predict her grades or her likelihood of graduating from high school. But do we agree on how to construct a just educational system or even an equitable classroom?

We believe one struggle that impedes us as a community of educators in our quest to create more just schools is a pattern of trying to solve complex problems or address complex conditions with simple, immediate solutions. Consider, for example, the time and resources schools across the U.S. have invested in attempting to narrow achievement gaps by training their teachers on culture- or identity-specific "learning styles"; on the "girl brain" and "boy brain"; on the "culture of poverty." We understand the lure of these approaches, as dangerous as they are. We share the sense of urgency that accompanies rooms full of students who cannot wait, and should not have to wait, for the educational revolution to come along before their learning needs are addressed more effectively.

Although easy practical solutions might be convenient, they also can do damage. Often they shift the equity responsibility onto the student, focusing on fixing students' mindsets or grittiness instead of addressing the conditions that require some students to be more resilient than others. They are simple and straightforward and, unfortunately, often more a *reflection of* inequity than a *challenge to* inequity.

For example, research has shown that teaching to particular learning styles is ineffective because students' learning styles and learning needs change depending on what they are learning, the context in which they're learning, from whom they are learning, and their confidence with the material, among other factors. Moreover, identity-specific learning styles simply *do not exist*. At any moment the diversity of preferred learning modalities *within* individual identity groups—African American boys, for example—is just as great as the diversity of preferred learning modalities *between* identity groups.

Complicating matters, a considerable portion of disparities in educational outcomes such as academic performance and graduation rates are symptoms of conditions that fall outside our individual spheres of influence as educators. We cannot control the racism and xenophobia students and their families face outside schools. We can and, we would argue, we *should* at the very least be aware of these conditions and how they affect students' lives and school experiences. After all, these conditions also affect students' interactions with us and with the schools in which we work.

Upon reading the scenario involving South Dovetown, it might be easy to think, *I have no control over the results of an election or bias in the community. That has nothing to do with school.* If only matters of diversity and social justice education were that simple.

When the meeting was almost over and Mr. Smith hadn't mentioned the election or the bias incidents, Ms. Samaya decided to speak up. As soon as Mr. Smith asked whether anybody had new business, she raised her hand.

"I think we need to talk about how this election is affecting our students," she said. Several of her colleagues nodded. A few others fidgeted uncomfortably in their seats. "Moreover," she added, "I think we need to take a stand against bias and bigotry. We need to let students know they are all welcome here. I don't know or care who voted for whom, but can't we at least agree we have a responsibility to all our students?"

As a wave of chatter filled the room Mr. Smith tried to regain control of the conversation. "OK, OK," he said loudly. "Let's settle down.

I figured somebody was going to bring that up. We are planning an anti-bullying workshop for our next professional development day. So things are in motion."

"What about a public statement? We need to let the community know we don't support all this bigotry," Ms. Samaya said.

Mr. Smith responded, "As for that, we need to be careful not to enter the political fray. As a school we can't take a political stand. We strive to be welcoming to all students, but a public statement might offend people who voted for Mayor Barton."

"Well, I voted for Mayor Barton and it would definitely offend me," Ms. Allister, a language arts teacher, said angrily. "Whatever happened to free speech? I feel like I can't be honest about how this influx of Somalis and Hispanics has made it harder to teach the kids who are actually from this community. And a lot of it goes back to their parents refusing to learn how to speak English."

There are no perfect answers or solutions when it comes to the complexities of diversity and social justice. Nobody has invented a magic formula for solving the issues swirling around South Dovetown. The scarcity of right answers underlines why we must develop and hone the knowledge and skills that help us to make sense of real-life messiness. Otherwise we risk allowing ourselves to be swayed by popular mythology and how we've been socialized to buy into that mythology when we respond to bias and inequity. We risk responding without an intricate understanding for why certain conditions exist in our classrooms and schools.

So, what would you do if you were Ms. Samaya or one of Ms. Samaya's colleagues attending that meeting? What would you do in the immediate term? Would you challenge Principal Smith or Ms. Allister? Would you attempt to invite others at the meeting into a conversation about why an anti-bullying workshop sometime in the future is not an adequate response? Would you look for other ways to support Somali and Central American students?

Just as importantly, how would you respond in the longer term, knowing others in the room might share Ms. Allister's beliefs or Mr. Smith's misunderstandings? How might you seek and share deeper insights about how Mayor Barton's election might affect students in the long run? How would you use what you learn to become a more equitable educator, not just for current students, but for future students?

Certainly, as much as we might want to do so, we cannot in our roles as educators control some of the bigger life situations in which our students and their families find themselves. We might not have the power in our roles as educators to eliminate racism and xenophobia from society; we probably don't have the power to change the fact that students will come to school with biases they learned from their parents or from the media. We *do*, however, have the power to understand how our students' lives outside of school—the repressions they and their families face, the inequities with which they contend—inform the way they experience us and school. We have the power to strengthen our abilities to create equitable learning environments and to maintain high expectations for all students by considering these contextual factors in addition to the everyday practicalities of our work as we shape our professional practice. We have the power to offer students new options for how to interpret what they see and hear.

The Case Method

One tool—in our experience, a particularly effective one—for strengthening these abilities is commonly called the "case method." The premise of the case method is, by analyzing real-life scenarios based on actual events, such as the situation at South Dovetown, we can practice applying theoretical ideas (like *educational equity*) to on-the-ground professional practice (Darling-Hammond, 2006). The case method enables us to practice stepping through a process of considering a range of perspectives and angles, to practice seeing the full complexity of school and classroom situations, and, as a result, to consider in a more focused manner how we might respond. In this sense, in the words of William and Margaret Naumes (1999), the case method is an "active pedagogical practice" (p. 11), an applicative process designed to build our capacities for evaluating and implementing mindful responses to complex, and often inequitable, school and classroom conditions (Leonard & Cook, 2010). In fact, studies have demonstrated the case method's effectiveness in deepening critical thinking abilities, problem-solving skills, and other competencies in professionals from a variety of fields, including neuroscience (Rosenbaum et al., 2014), nursing (Mills et al., 2014), food studies (Gallego et al., 2013), and of course education (Bonney, 2015; Brown & Kraehe, 2010).

Richard Foster and his colleagues (2010) explain, in this spirit, the nature of a case method "case":

> The teaching case is a story, a narrative if you will, usually based on actual events and told with a definite teaching purpose. It does not have a correct answer or obvious solution, relying instead on the nature of the real world where answers are difficult to come by and solutions are always contested. [We] are introduced to the need to think carefully, to listen to the points made by others and to evaluate those arguments, to review alternative courses of action and their efficacy, and to interpret real-world experience. (p. 523)

This, we think, is among the most formidable challenges the case method poses to current and future educators. In this era of high-stakes testing and standardization, when many of us feel increasingly desperate for practical solutions to complex problems, the idea that there usually isn't a practical solution or "right answer" can be daunting. The point of examining cases like those in this book is not to be constrained by boxes—*this* is correct, so *this* must be incorrect—but rather to muddle through the gray areas by considering all that makes them gray. The case method allows us to do this in a way that few other pedagogical methods allow. This is how it helps us grow our *equity literacy*, as we will discuss in Chapter 2.

The muddling is especially important when it comes to matters of diversity and social justice. After all, none of us wants to contribute to racial, or class, or gender injustices in our classrooms. We want all the students at South Dovetown to succeed, to be protected from racism, heterosexism, xenophobia, and other forms of oppression. The trouble is, we might not always understand how we help to create some of the barriers to their learning, despite our philosophical commitments to equity and justice.

The other important diversity and social justice benefit of the case method is that it challenges us to question our own mental models by examining classroom situations through a variety of lenses

(Gallucci, 2006). It challenges us to practice asking the questions we might never have thought to ask; to reconsider old ways of thinking in light of new understandings. How do we see the situation at Dovetown differently when we let go of old notions that conflate anti-bullying efforts with equity and justice efforts or old ways of looking at things that mark inaction as apolitical and action as political? How might we think differently about ourselves as equitable and just educators when we learn better how to see past our presumptions and consider a broader picture? These are the sorts of questions that cannot be answered by theory alone or by memorizing "five practical strategies for teaching all immigrant students." They require deeper, more critical, reflection: the kind encouraged by the case method.

With this in mind, we chose to write *Case Studies on Diversity and Social Justice Education* for several reasons. Firstly, especially since writing the first edition of this book, we have observed how the case method strengthens our efforts to prepare educators, including us, to think, teach, lead, and advocate more equitably and justly. As educators we have experienced situations similar to those described in our cases but have found too few opportunities to process what has happened as mindfully as possible. These cases provide an opportunity to practice doing just that.

Additionally, as we mentioned earlier, when we haven't practiced, it can be particularly challenging for us to "see" what is happening in our classrooms and schools unconstrained by our existing biases and ideologies. The case method provides opportunities to bolster these abilities by practicing thoughtful analysis and problem-solving skills. We have constructed the cases purposefully to challenge ourselves and our readers to consider our teaching in light of what Nieto and Bode (2011) call the *sociopolitical context of schooling*. Taking account of this sociopolitical context requires us to recognize the relationship between the inequities plaguing our schools and larger societal inequities, even when we don't see those larger conditions as within our sphere of influence.

It is our hope this book will create this kind of deeper reflection about equity, diversity, and social justice concerns in schools and, by doing so, encourage readers to consider how they might ensure *all* students have the opportunity to excel.

The Rest of This Book

Without question, the essence of this book is in the cases themselves: 42 scenarios approximating actual school and classroom events we have witnessed ourselves or heard about from colleagues. Each case, written in a narrative style, presents a complex yet fairly common school or classroom scenario in which an injustice—sometimes implicit, sometimes explicit—might be in play. It is up to you, the reader, to weigh the situation and decide how to respond. Issues include racism and white privilege; sexism, transphobia, and male- and cis-privilege; heterosexism and heteronormativity; poverty and economic injustice; language bias and linguicism; religious-based oppression; and various intersections of these and other conditions.

In order to encourage the complex analysis we believe best prepares us to understand and respond to inequitable classroom and school conditions, we follow this Introduction, in Chapter 2, by outlining a case analysis process constructed and honed through our combined decades' worth of teaching and teacher professional development experience. We also step back through the case incorporated into this Introduction to demonstrate how to apply the case analysis process.

Chapters 3 through 11 contain cases specific to particular identities and oppressions. Each case includes a section of facilitator notes—we call them "Points for Consideration"—comprised of recommendations for issues and concepts that can be highlighted and explored. These can be found in Appendix B. This unique feature provides valuable insights for understanding the cases' nuances and for applying important concepts to the analysis process. Each case also includes a series of questions intended to encourage deep, informed reflection. We should mention that the division of the cases into identity-based chapters is imprecise. Most cases address multiple identities and oppressions.

Finally, although we specify in some cases whether they occurred in an elementary, middle, or high school, most of the cases are written to be applicable across age groups.

2

ANALYZING CASES USING THE EQUITY LITERACY FRAMEWORK

The trouble with most school diversity and social justice education initiatives is not so much a shortage of strategies or approaches for making classrooms and schools more equitable and just. We often feel buried in strategies and approaches. If it's not the now-debunked focus on "learning styles," it's "grit." If it's not "grit" it's the "mindset of poverty." If it's not that, it's just about anything else that enables us to step gingerly around real conversations about issues like racism, heterosexism, and ableism in schools.

Neither is the problem a scarcity of people who appreciate diversity. We can point to unapologetic bigots in every field, including education. In our experience, though, most educators appreciate diversity at least philosophically and very few exhibit explicit bigotry.

Instead, in our experience, the trouble is the familiar cycle of educators and schools adopting simplistic, ineffective strategies and approaches for attending to diversity that pose no threat to inequity. We might appreciate diversity, but that appreciation by itself does not prepare us to cultivate equity in our classrooms and schools. So we adopt and apply a steady stream of strategies and build a variety of initiatives for "closing" the "achievement gap," but do we understand the conditions that underlie the "achievement gap" well enough to build initiatives that respond to them adequately? Do we see how the thing we call an achievement gap is more aptly described as an *opportunity gap*? This is important, because if we can't see the opportunity gap, we have no real shot at eliminating the achievement gap.

We wrote this book to help you, the reader, practice this kind of seeing.

Equity Literacy Framework

Our goal was to use case study or case scenario pedagogy to provide an engaging vehicle for posing the kinds of questions that help strengthen educators' *equity literacy* (Gorski & Swalwell, 2015; Swalwell, 2011)— educators' *literacy* related to *equity*. In the most basic terms equity literacy refers to the knowledge and skills we need as educators to be a threat to the existence of bias and inequity in our spheres of influence (Gorski, 2016, 2017). It refers to the knowledge and skills that prepare us, not to fix the cultures or mindsets of this or that group of students, not merely to appreciate diversity, but to root bias and inequity out of our classrooms, schools, and communities.

This is what sets equity literacy apart from cultural competence, intercultural relations, and many other popular frameworks for attending to diversity in schools. It encourages us to understand dynamics related to, say, race or gender identity, not just in terms of interpersonal or cultural conflict, but also as part of bigger, broader social and cultural conditions. When we develop our equity literacy, we naturally filter every decision through an equity lens. We begin to recognize subtle biases and inequities we previously didn't see. And we don't just recognize them. We understand them and our roles as educators as parts of a bigger equity and justice context. It's not about doing a bunch of new things, necessarily, like adding new strategies to our existing mental filebook of strategies. Instead it's about developing the ability to do everything we do with equity in mind.

Thinking back to South Dovetown Middle School, the principal, Mr. Smith, dismissed Ms. Samaya's recommendation that the school should make a public statement asserting its commitment to being welcoming for all students. He reasoned such a statement might offend people who voted for Mayor Barton, who had rallied his base in part by demonizing immigrants. Making a public statement is a political act, he argued, and Dovetown should not enter the political fray.

It might be easy to read Principal Smith's reaction as reasonable or even as diversity-conscious. He doesn't want to alienate families who voted for Mr. Barton. They are part of the school community, too. And remember, he did initiate plans for an anti-bullying workshop. Certainly, many people working in schools could use help recognizing and responding to bullying.

On the other hand, if we apply an equity literacy lens and do a deep diversity and social justice dive into the situation at Dovetown, we might see things differently. There's something deeper, more complex, going on in this scenario. Bullying is a symptom of that something, not the core issue. The something involves broader social conditions and privilege, racial entitlement, and institutional culture. It involves what we see or don't see as "political." There is no way to work through any of this diversity and social justice messiness with an anti-bullying workshop and a vague institutional philosophy of being "welcoming." Principal Smith might be applying what he imagines to be an equity strategy, but it's an equity strategy that, alone, is no threat to inequity. Equity literacy is the ability to make this distinction.

This is why we decided to create a new process for examining equity-related education cases and crafting responses to the problems they pose, grounding that process in the equity literacy framework. The equity literacy framework is constructed to move us into the messiness. It forces us to simultaneously consider concerns as micro-level as our individual biases and ideologies and as macro-level as structural racism and heteronormativity. It challenges us to reflect upon how our instructional, leadership, or other decisions affect students and how life experiences outside school also affect them. As a result, it positions us to respond to classroom challenges involving matters of diversity and social justice in more nuanced, just, and transformative ways.

The four foundational abilities of equity literacy, which are incorporated into the case analysis process described below, are summarized in Table 2.1. This book and the case analysis approach are designed to help readers cultivate these abilities in ourselves and in one another.

Table 2.1 The four abilities of equity literacy

EQUITY LITERACY ABILITIES	EXAMPLES OF ASSOCIATED SKILLS AND DISPOSITIONS
Ability to *recognize* even the subtlest biases and inequities	Equity literate educators: • notice even subtle bias in classroom materials, classroom interactions, and school policies; and • reject deficit views that locate the sources of outcome inequalities (such as test score or graduate rate disparities) as existing within students' "mindsets" or "cultures" rather than as resulting from disparate levels of access to resources and experiences in and out of school.
Ability to *respond to* biases and inequities in the immediate term	Equity literate educators: • have the facilitation skills and content knowledge needed to intervene effectively when biases or inequities, such as gender bias or sexism, arise in classrooms, faculty meetings, or other contexts; and • foster conversations with colleagues about bias and inequity concerns at their schools.
Ability to *redress* biases and inequities in the long term	Equity literate educators: • advocate against inequitable school practices, such as racially or economically biased tracking, and advocate for equitable school practices; and • identify ways to mitigate structural barriers—lack of access to preventive healthcare, for example—that impede educational engagement by replacing school or classroom practices that exacerbate these barriers with practices designed to weaken their impact.
Ability to *create and sustain* a bias-free and equitable learning environment	Equity literate educators: • express high expectations for all students through higher-order pedagogies and curricula; and • demonstrate a willingness to withstand complaints about changes meant to redistribute educational access and opportunity more equitably.

Source: Adapted from Paul Gorski's *Reaching and Teaching Students in Poverty: Strategies for Erasing the Opportunity Gap* (forthcoming in 2018)

Case Analysis: An Equity Literacy Process

Our process for analyzing educational cases, assembled to strengthen in educators the four abilities of equity literacy, is comprised of seven steps, summarized in Figure 2.1. The steps are accumulative, designed

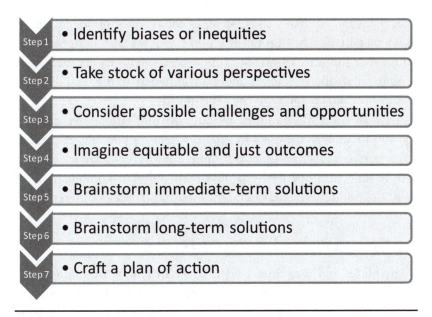

Step 1 • Identify biases or inequities

Step 2 • Take stock of various perspectives

Step 3 • Consider possible challenges and opportunities

Step 4 • Imagine equitable and just outcomes

Step 5 • Brainstorm immediate-term solutions

Step 6 • Brainstorm long-term solutions

Step 7 • Craft a plan of action

Figure 2.1 Seven steps in the equity literacy case analysis approach

to prepare us to develop informed, mindful responses to multilayered classroom and school scenarios. They move us through a process of peeling away layers of the proverbial onion, never settling for quick, simple responses that rely too heavily on our predispositions or presuppositions.

In what follows we describe each of the seven steps of the equity literacy case analysis process. Hoping to demonstrate the process in action, we apply the steps to the scenario at South Dovetown Middle School described in Chapter 1. (An abbreviated, printable version of the process can be found in Appendix A.)

As you will see, the case analysis process is not designed to guide you toward a *correct* set of strategies for responding to and redressing the conditions at Dovetown or described in the other cases. Hand this process and any of these cases to ten teachers or school administrators and chances are they will produce ten different action plans. Instead, we designed the process to help you practice using your unique insights, your knowledge about students and their families, and your expertise with school and classroom dynamics in order to respond, as effectively and equitably as possible, to the types of biases and inequities that inevitably crop up in schools. But we also designed it to infuse your insights, knowledge, and expertise with equity literacy. It is more an art than a science; more a willingness to dig, and dig, and dig deeply than an ability to calculate quickly.

This also is why, humbled by our own limitations, we encourage you to analyze the cases in groups whenever possible. Almost as important as reflecting upon our unique individual analyses of each case is reflecting upon why people with different combinations of identities and life experiences might interpret the cases differently.

Step 1: Identify Biases or Inequities Posed by the Case

Many biases and inequities students face in school are implicit and unintentional, hidden in day-to-day practices, school traditions, and quiet interactions. It can be especially difficult to recognize the sorts of challenges students or families face when we have never faced those challenges ourselves. If you have never been the target of racism and xenophobia or watched a public figure encourage prejudice against people in your family or community, it might be difficult to understand Ms. Samaya's sense of urgency for the school to respond explicitly to the aftermath of the election. So we urge you during Step 1 to read between the lines. Practice *recognizing* conditions and contexts you might not usually recognize or seeing what you might be conditioned not to see.

Begin by naming biases, inequities, or otherwise troublesome conditions that are immediately apparent to you. For some readers, perhaps it is apparent and troublesome that at least one teacher, Ms. Allister, is minimizing biased or prejudiced views as "free speech" without considering that, free as it might be, prejudiced language and ideas still have an impact on her students. She also appears resentful of the growing population of Somali and Central American immigrants at the school. Is it possible her resentment is affecting her engagement with these students and their families? Can she feel this resentment and also demonstrate high expectations for them? What are the chances several other teachers feel the same as Ms. Allister but aren't saying so?

Once you have a grasp of the more surface-level dynamics, dig deeper. Look for less explicit, not-so-obvious examples of existing or potential bias, inequity, stereotypes, or presumptions. What does the case tell us about school or classroom policy, about instructional or leadership practices, about individuals' attitudes and perspectives that might hint at something deeper than surface-level biases and inequities? Consider, for example, what some readers might interpret as Principal Smith's dismissive tone regarding Ms. Samaya's concerns, or his failure to address the issue without Ms. Samaya's prompting. We might also scrutinize his decision to respond to a string of bias incidents only with anti-bullying training when the incidents reflect not just the acts of isolated bullies, but growing sentiments in the community.

Remember, there are no right or wrong answers here—no single "problem" that everybody should identify. Different people will identify different problems, and that's fine. In fact, it's an opportunity for us to learn from one another what we tend to see and what we might tend to miss.

Step 2: Take Stock of Varying Perspectives

Our case has at least a couple of obvious stakeholders who might have different perspectives on what is happening. Most obvious, perhaps, are the people directly involved in the exchange: Ms. Samaya, Ms. Allister, and Principal Smith. In the most immediate term, we might note that our colleague, Ms. Samaya, has probably been hurt by both the principal's inaction and Ms. Allister's comments. We might try to put ourselves in her shoes and consider how she could be experiencing the interaction.

But we shouldn't stop there. Ms. Samaya might be the only person who spoke up, but that doesn't necessarily mean she's the only person present at the meeting who could be concerned about the principal's silence or Ms. Allister's comments. In every case we should consider, not only the people immediately involved, but also those within earshot and eyeshot. Even those present who were not offended by Ms. Allister's comments or who agreed with Ms. Allister's assessment of the situation have a stake in the outcome. What happens next will send a message to *everybody* in the room about what Principal Smith values. Even if his next move simply confirms some people's existing ideas instead of challenging them, that's significant enough to note.

Complicating matters, despite being at the center of the scenario, the people attending the meeting are not the only people with a stake in the outcome. The Somali and Central American students and their families have perspectives. Is the school going to reproduce the conditions they experience in the community or challenge those conditions? The school's decision whether to respond explicitly or not will affect the entire community. Moreover, even if Principal Smith eventually chooses against institutional silence and supports a public statement, students carry what they experience outside school into schools and classrooms. As educators who value equity and justice, we have to be responsive to what students carry into school with them even if we do not have the power to eliminate every structural barrier they experience outside schools.

Again, dig deeply. The idea is to challenge our own thinking. For example, this is an important consideration: although the principal believes making a public statement will throw the school into the political fray, it's also true that deciding not to respond is *just as political* an act as responding. Silence has as much impact as outspokenness. Who would be impacted most by the silence?

We encourage you to seek balance between focusing only on the most obvious stakeholders and broadening your focus so much that the discussion becomes unwieldy. Start with the immediate participants and then, at the very least, the ring of constituents around them. Focus both on marginalized communities and privileged communities.

We realize this step requires speculating. There is no real way for us to know what somebody else's perspective is. We can, however, challenge ourselves to try to see the incident through a variety of lenses.

Step 3: Consider Possible Challenges and Opportunities

Given the varied perspectives explored in Step 2, our next task is to identify potential challenges and opportunities presented by the situation. Start with the individuals involved. Ms. Samaya has already identified an opportunity. Dovetown can choose to make a positive, equity-informed statement letting families who might be experiencing bias know they are welcome at the school. There's a more general opportunity for every educator at Dovetown to learn more about the challenges and barriers with which their students contend, to learn about how forms of racism and xenophobia that exist outside school often are replicated inside school. These are lessons they can apply to other students who might experience bias and inequity, such as low-income students or lesbian, gay, or bisexual students, or transgender students. Certainly in the immediate term an opportunity has arisen to help Ms. Allister develop more equitable beliefs about a significant proportion of her students.

Of course, the scenario also presents several challenges we need to consider as we work toward solutions. Ms. Allister's views present a significant challenge, along with the probability that she is not alone in her biased beliefs. Another challenge might revolve around finding ways to respond constructively to student bias and bigotry when that bias and bigotry likely have been taught at home. Principal Smith's apparent aversion to controversy and resulting willingness to prioritize the comfort of families who voted for Mayor Barton over the comfort and safety of students whose families are the targets of bias and injustice, also presents a challenge because he has the most power at the school.

Moving further into the messiness, even if Principal Smith is missing the equity mark in this regard, his concern over the politics of the situation can be insightful. Certainly we must consider how supporters of Mayor Barton might react if the school responds more boldly than offering anti-bullying professional development. The school *should* do something more and *should* prepare itself for possible fallout. We will need to consider that preparation in Steps 5, 6, and 7.

Remember to use your analysis from Steps 1 and 2 to inform your assessment of challenges and opportunities. In later steps the goal will be to *respond to* and *redress* the equity problems posed by cases while also taking optimal advantage of the opportunities the cases present for individual and institutional growth.

Step 4: Imagine Equitable Outcomes

Building on the contextual understandings we have gained by taking stock of stakeholders' perspectives and considering possible challenges and opportunities, we begin imagining positive and equitable outcomes. This is a critical step, as Steps 5 through 7 are designed to filter all the thinking and analyzing we have done so far into solutions meant to reach the outcomes we imagine in Step 4.

A few guiding principles can be helpful as we imagine what we hope to achieve by resolving the cases in this book. First, it's important to distinguish *equitable* outcomes from *equal* outcomes. As we see it, equality connotes *sameness*. Equity, on the other hand, connotes *fairness*, a redistribution of access and opportunity, including access to a bias-free, supportive, actively anti-racist, anti-sexist, anti-heterosexist, anti-transphobic, anti-ableist, anti-every-other-oppression educational experience. Equity takes context into account. The equality-minded educator might think, hey, we need to value all children all the time, so responding so directly to Mayor Barton's election and its aftermath sends the wrong message that we care more about immigrant students than other students. All students experience barriers, they might say, so why focus so much on one or two specific groups and their challenges? The equity-literate educator might acknowledge, yes, all students experience barriers, but all students don't experience racism and xenophobia on top of the other barriers. We have to redistribute energies and resources to address a form of injustice harming a particular group of students especially harshly right now. Sometimes equity is unequal. And vice versa.

Secondly, remember to think both *immediate term* and *long term*. What can be resolved right now, on the spot, and what will equity look like once it is resolved? Imagine yourself in the room with the Dovetown staff. How would you intervene in the moment? Would you challenge Principal Smith on the "politics" justification for refusing Ms. Samaya's suggestion? Would you invite your colleagues into a conversation about what might be useful beyond anti-bullying training? How might you respond to Ms. Allister?

Consider long-term outcomes, as well. Perhaps an equitable outcome would include anti-racism and anti-xenophobic professional development on top of the anti-bullying training for everybody at Dovetown, including Principal Smith. It might also include a set of policy initiatives to guide how to respond to future situations similar to the one in which the school is currently embroiled.

Finally, *be specific*. Identify very specific, on-the-ground outcomes. How, specifically, will things be different in the school or classroom if we commit to resolving the issue and all its nuances equitably?

Step 5: Brainstorm Immediate-Term Responses

Now that you have some equitable outcomes in mind, we begin brainstorming strategies to get us there. What are some of the things we might do *right now* to achieve those outcomes if we were educators at Dovetown? This is a brainstorm, remember, so don't overthink. Focus on using the understandings that you've developed in Steps 1 through 4 and, of course, your own experience and expertise, and make a list. You'll have an opportunity in Step 7 to refine your ideas into a formal action plan.

Step 6: Brainstorm Longer-Term Policy and Practice Adjustments

In Step 6 we develop longer-term strategies, often for more substantive change. This is where we might brainstorm ways to bolster awareness about the sorts of challenges the Somali and Central American students experience in and out of school. It is where we focus on shifting institutional culture and knowledge, infusing equity into school-wide policies and practices or even district policies and practices, if we believe they need to be altered to achieve our equitable outcomes.

Here, again, we're brainstorming. Try not to self-censor. Record whatever ideas come to mind based on Steps 1 through 5.

Step 7: Craft a Plan of Action

During the final step we craft our brainstorms into specific actions we believe will result in the equitable outcomes we outlined in Step 5. What would we do in the immediate term? What would we do that might be a little longer-term equity project? How would we respond to ensure, to the best of our knowledge and power, justice for everybody involved?

A Few Final Thoughts

We recognize that in the heat of the moment we do not have time to sit down and think through the seven steps of a case analysis process. The point is not to memorize these steps or to step through them carefully at every instance of inequity.

Instead, the idea is to use them to practice our equity literacy skills by reflecting on classroom and school conditions through a social justice lens. Use them to practice grappling with the nuances and complexities inherent in any institution full of people with different aspirations and gifts and challenges in a society full of bias and injustice. For additional guidance refer to the "Points for Consideration" for each case in Appendix B. These points offer valuable insight we might otherwise miss when analyzing a case.

Practice enough and that equity view will become second nature. We begin to see the nuances and complexities previously invisible, or at least a little hazy, to us. That is how we cultivate equity literacy—how we become a threat to the existence of bias and inequity in our spheres of influence.

3

CASES ON POVERTY AND SOCIOECONOMIC STATUS

CASE 3.1: CHOCOLATE BAR FUNDRAISER

The Parent Teacher Association (PTA) at Broadway School had for years organized fundraisers to defray the effects of budget cuts or to raise money so student groups could participate in out-of-town events. Many of these fundraisers revolved around students selling something—usually chocolate bars. Students who sold the most goods were rewarded with passes to theme parks and other prizes, including recognition at an all school assembly.

So at the first PTA meeting of the school year, when Ms. Alexander, the mother of a Broadway student, raised a concern about its plan to run such a fundraiser, she caught several other attendees by surprise. "We've been doing this for years," Ms. Torrence, the PTA president, said, "and nobody's ever had a problem with it. What are your concerns?"

Ms. Alexander, a single mother who struggled financially despite working two jobs, explained, "This school isn't like it used to be, when most students were from well-to-do families. There are more kids here, like my son, whose families and neighbors can't afford to buy boxes of candy bars. It's embarrassing, with other students talking about how much their own families have purchased."

Ms. Torrence nodded sympathetically, then asked whether anybody else had concerns about the fundraiser. Mr. Cuertas, whose daughter attended Broadway, raised his hand. "My daughter felt awful last year when she couldn't sell many candy bars. I don't think we should set up students for embarrassment or depend on them to raise money."

Ms. Torrence was sensitive to the growing numbers of low-income students attending Broadway. She had made what she considered great effort to increase PTA participation among lower-income parents. She sent postcards and placed phone calls to almost every family and even offered dinner at meetings. These efforts helped increase participation, but unfortunately, as far as she could tell, Ms. Alexander and Mr. Cuertas were the only two lower-income parents out of the 20-or-so people attending the meeting that night. She appreciated that they were speaking up, but was worried about how other attendees might respond.

Before Ms. Torrence could respond to Ms. Alexander and Mr. Cuertas, Ms. Plumlee said, "So, we're not going to let any students do this fundraiser because a few kids might feel bad? Bottom line is that we need the money for programs that benefit *all* students. This fundraiser has worked in the past and not everyone has to participate."

Mr. Winterstein agreed, adding, "My son sold the second most chocolate bars last year. He worked hard, going door to door and emailing friends and relatives. If these kids worked harder, they could sell as many chocolate bars as he sold."

Ms. Plumlee added, "If other families care so much, maybe they should come to these meetings. We have to decide with who is here, so let's just take a vote."

Ms. Plumlee was correct: the group usually voted on issues on which they didn't reach consensus. She called for a vote, which meant, technically speaking, Ms. Torrence was supposed to facilitate a vote. She hesitated, however, empathizing with Ms. Alexander and Mr. Cuertas and feeling that their concerns remained unresolved.

Questions

1 What are the equity implications of fundraisers that require students to sell items such as chocolate bars? Do you agree with Ms. Alexander's concerns about how these fundraisers can alienate students experiencing poverty? Why or why not?

2 If the PTA members are intent on raising funds to support student activities or make up for budget cuts, what are some ways in which they can do so that might not require students to compete

with one another? How else might the PTA go about addressing the lack of funding for student activities?

3 Ms. Torrence knew the concerns raised by Ms. Alexander and Mr. Cuertas would be drowned out by the voices of other meeting attendees who saw the chocolate bar fundraiser as a school tradition. Can you think of other examples of school traditions that, despite being supported by many people, are biased against or inequitable toward some students and families?

CASE 3.2: THE TROUBLE WITH GRIT

Samantha, a student at Hillside School, loves science. "Are we doing lab work today?" she often asks Ms. Grady as she hurries into science class. She usually aces quizzes and tests and even helps classmates with their work.

So Ms. Grady can't understand why Samantha rarely turns in homework. She knows Samantha's family is experiencing poverty, so her first impulse was to wonder whether there were issues at home. She has reached out to colleagues who teach Samantha's younger siblings to inquire whether they notice similar patterns. She learned Samantha's younger siblings always turn in their homework.

Ms. Grady also has reached out to Samantha every way she knows how, pleading with her. "You could have an A if you did your homework! You have the smarts, now you need to show that you have the grit." She has reached out to Samantha's parents, too. She has called the phone number they provided the school, but nobody answers.

Imagine how successful Samantha could be if her parents helped support her, Ms. Grady has thought. She has grown increasingly frustrated trying to support Samantha. She has dozens of other students who also need attention, most without Samantha's natural gifts. And her grading policy is clear: failure to turn in homework results in a grade of "0." If she bends her policy for Samantha, she believes, she risks being unfair to other students.

One day after school Ms. Grady approaches Mr. Burns, a language arts teacher who also has Samantha in class. "I've tried to reach her parents," she explains, "but they never respond. Don't they care about her grades?"

"I had the same experience. I didn't know what to think until I visited them at home," Mr. Burns replies.

It never occurred to Ms. Grady to visit Samantha's home. "What did you learn?"

"A *lot*," he answers, explaining how Samantha lives with a single mother who works multiple jobs, beginning her day at 5 a.m. on a restaurant cleaning crew and ending around 9:30 p.m. on another cleaning crew. She usually returns around 10 p.m., trying not to wake the kids.

"So that's why Samantha struggles with homework. The moment she's home from school she's helping her siblings until they go to bed," Mr. Burns explains.

"Poor thing," Ms. Grady replies. "Her mother is not helping Samantha develop the grit and mindset needed to break their cycle of poverty."

Mr. Burns, who had grown up in poverty, was uncomfortable with how Ms. Grady was characterizing the problem: as irresponsibility on Samantha's mother's part and as a lack of grit on Samantha's part. He knew the situation was more complex than that, but couldn't quite find words to articulate his concern. He also knew Ms. Grady was not alone in her beliefs about Samantha's family and other families experiencing poverty. He worried the school's new focus on "grit" would contribute to their misunderstandings.

He wanted to respond productively, but how?

Questions

1 An *equality* view dictates we treat all students equally. This is the view Ms. Grady has applied to her homework policy when it comes to Samantha. How might her perspective change if she adopted an *equity* view instead, taking stock of the barriers and challenges individual students experience and crafting policy to be responsive to those barriers and challenges?

2 Do you agree with Ms. Grady that Samantha is displaying a lack of grit by not turning in her homework? Why or why not? In what ways is Samantha demonstrating grit and resilience?

3 Mr. Burns worries that Ms. Grady and several of his other colleagues have a deficit view of families experiencing poverty, tending to attribute conditions like Samantha not turning in her homework to supposed deficiencies in those families. How might taking the deficit view force us into misunderstandings of the challenges and barriers students like Samantha face at school?

CASE 3.3: STUDENT PROTEST

Melody and Javier, seniors at North Shore High School, had attended Burlington County Public Schools (BCPS) since Kindergarten. They attended elementary and middle school together at the lowest-income schools in the district. During their years in BCPS they experienced growing class sizes, a heightened focus on high-stakes testing, and the erosion of music and arts programs.

A couple years earlier, as a project for civics class, Melody and Javier attempted to organize a peaceful protest against deteriorating conditions at North Shore. Their teacher, Ms. Tilston, was a strong advocate for civic engagement. She often ended class with students brainstorming what they could do to create a better world based on what they were studying in class. In final assignment of the school year, she asked students to pick one social issue and propose a plan for creating a better world. Melody and Javier were not satisfied with *proposing* a plan. They wanted to experience protesting, but Ms. Tilston quashed the idea. "I love your spirit," she said, "but I don't want you getting into trouble."

Now, two years later, news began circulating that BCPS intended to close North Shore. The district had been losing students and, under state pressure, decided to consolidate schools. North Shore, which had the lowest test scores among the district's high schools, was on the chopping block.

Though staff were asked to refrain from speaking about the closure until the plan for redistribution was announced, there was a lot of chatter as the situation was all over local news. Many students were angry. They knew this wouldn't happen to a school full of wealthier students.

Melody and Javier decided it was time to organize the protest they started planning a couple years earlier, so they asked Ms. Tilston for support. "I suggest that you do a little research. Read about protests students have done in other districts. Surround yourself with others who feel like you do."

They followed her advice and invited other students to a meeting outside school. The students decided they'd divide into groups, each taking on a specific task, then meet again in a couple days.

When they did meet again they decided they would organize a peaceful walkout by marching a couple blocks, then line the sidewalk along the boulevard, holding signs and chanting their displeasure. In the meantime their most important task was to spread the word about the walkout and to remind everybody it would be a *peaceful* protest. "Make sure to tell everyone, no cursing or violence," Melody told the group.

They scheduled the walkout for the following Wednesday, 10 a.m. When Javier saw Melody the morning of the walkout he asked whether she noticed the extra police presence around school. "How could I miss it?" she answered.

Ms. Tilston noticed it, too, and it frightened her. She knew the students had their plan together. But she worried the police presence would elevate tensions. As she sat at her desk wondering what to do, Javier and Melody appeared at her classroom door.

Questions

1 Do you agree with the decision to ask teachers not to speak with students about the school consolidation plan while district administrators decided where they would send the students the following year? Why or why not?

2 If you were Ms. Tilston, and Melody and Javier approached you for advice about how to funnel their frustrations into positive action, what would you have suggested they do? How involved in their plans would you want to be? What repercussions could exist for your decision if you choose to get involved?

3 School closings can have detrimental effects on local communities. Why might school closures in low-income areas have especially detrimental effects on the students and families in those communities?

CASE 3.4: HIGH EXPECTATIONS OR UNREALISTIC GOALS?

Ms. Sutter was excited to form an after-school club at Pinewood School for students who could become the first people in their families to attend college. She started seeing a need for such a club as she noticed many of her students lacked knowledge about post-secondary education. Though many of their parents encouraged them to think about college, her students did not have the same opportunities as wealthier peers to see a college campus or learn about post-secondary options.

Ms. Sutter proposed the club at a staff meeting. Some teachers thought it was unnecessary, but others were excited and offered support. A major point of discussion was the club's grade range. Should it be open to all students or limited to higher grade levels?

Ms. Bates, a second grade teacher, commented, "Experience tells me fifth grade is too early to start talking to *these* kids about college. It's way over their heads."

Another teacher, Ms. Clark, added, "Families in our school will enroll their children in any free after-school program just to keep them busy. You'll be swamped and end up spending more time on discipline than on college."

Ms. Sutter disagreed with her peers' opinions, but she reluctantly agreed to offer the club exclusively to fifth graders.

Several months later Ms. Sutter paused during her "College Club" meeting to marvel at how well it was going. Students attended regularly, and parents would arrive before pick-up time to join lively discussions about college life.

As a year-end celebration, Ms. Sutter scheduled a field trip to the renowned local university, which would include a guided tour. When they arrived on campus she asked the students to wait outside the admissions office while she went in to alert the receptionist the group had arrived. After speaking with the receptionist, Ms. Sutter was shocked to learn their assigned tour guide had been reassigned, as a result, her group would need to conduct a self-guided tour.

"But I didn't attend this university! I can't give them an adequate tour. Why not just let us join another group?" she implored.

"I'm sorry, but guides are prioritized for prospective, high school students," the receptionist responded. As Ms. Sutter continued to plead the club's case, she was approached by the Director of Admissions, Mr. Stein.

"Can I help you?" he asked warmly.

"Yes," responded Ms. Sutter. "I have a group of fifth graders here, potential first-generation college students," she said, before explaining how excited students were about the tour.

Mr. Stein asked Ms. Sutter to step into his office. *Wonderful!* thought Ms. Sutter. *Maybe he'll be the person who gives us a tour.*

Instead Mr. Stein said, "I'm sorry a tour guide is unavailable. We do our best to avoid these situations, but I have students here who are credible applicants. I can't compromise their interest by prioritizing fifth graders ahead of them." He paused briefly before adding, "Frankly, I worry you're getting your students excited about a place they probably will never attend. Perhaps you should be touring the community college."

With this, he opened his office door, inviting Ms. Sutter to leave. Ms. Sutter glanced through a window and saw her students waiting patiently for their tour. She fought back tears as she contemplated what to tell them and how to address Mr. Stein's prejudicial comments.

Questions

1 What advice would you have given Ms. Sutter when she was deciding which students should be permitted to participate in the club?

2 Ms. Sutter heard from multiple people, including Mr. Stein, that it was unnecessary to discuss a full range of post-secondary options with her students. To what extent, if at all, do you agree with this sentiment?

3 Mr. Stein expressed his concern about Ms. Sutter creating false excitement about a prestigious university. How would you have responded to Mr. Stein's comments?

CASE 3.5: TECHNOLOGY PROGRESS, EQUITY REGRESS

"Transitioning to a Technology Future": this was the theme school leaders at Oak Grove School chose entering the new school year. Once a school with a relatively wealthy student body, Oak Grove had changed demographically. The percentage of students on free or reduced price lunch had climbed to 45%.

Ms. Carmella, Oak Grove's principal, had decided this year the school would prioritize technology. Teachers would be required to incorporate computer and Internet technologies across the curriculum. The school would transition to an online platform for communicating with parents.

During staff orientation the week before students returned to school, Principal Carmella announced the plan and mentioned workshop opportunities to help staff integrate technology into their classes. She assured everyone time and support would be provided for reconstructing curricula, which seemed to be a concern for staff.

As the conversation wound down, Ms. Dehne, an Oak Grove teacher, worried an important point was being missed: as the number of students experiencing poverty at the school grew, so grew the number of families who did not have computers or Internet access at home. She also knew many of her colleagues responded defensively when she raised these sorts of concerns. The more she raised concerns about the experiences of these students, the more she felt she was labeled a "troublemaker." Still, she felt responsible for asking questions.

"I'm wondering how the families who don't have computers or Internet are going to access this new platform," she remarked. "And shouldn't we talk about how to avoid assigning homework and projects that require technology some of our students don't have?" she added.

"*Most* of our students have computers and Internet access at home," Ms. Gifford, another teacher, insisted, "so why should we spend time focusing on the few who don't? Besides, even our families who receive free or reduced lunch have cell phones with Internet access. I see students on their phones all the time in the hallways."

Principal Carmella chimed in, "Part of the benefit of this initiative is, we're inviting families to change with us. Students from lower socioeconomic backgrounds need this more than anyone if they don't want to be left behind. Our building is full of computers, and so is the local library. We can encourage students to use them after school."

Ms. Dehne agreed technology literacy was important for students, but she couldn't help but feel this initiative would unintentionally punish students whose families could not afford the resources necessary to participate fully. But after several instances of "learning the hard way," Ms. Dehne knew continuing to press her concerns in that moment would not be useful.

Questions

1 Principal Carmella suggested alternatives for students who did not have access to computers and Internet access at home. What barriers might make it difficult for students to take advantage of these alternatives? Can you think of other examples of technology-related initiatives or practices that might look like technological process while also threatening to expand access and opportunity gaps between families experiencing poverty and others?

2 What are some ways Oak Grove could adjust the initiatives laid out by Principal Carmella to avoid creating more inequity for students and families experiencing poverty? How can the school cultivate technology literacy among students without assigning homework or projects requiring its use?

3 Do you agree with Ms. Gifford's suggestion that, if most students at the school do have computer and Internet access (assuming she knows that to be true), Ms. Dehne should not focus so much on those who don't have access? Should policy and practice be created based on the access and opportunity enjoyed by *most* students even if it might disadvantage other students?

4

CASES ON RELIGION

CASE 4.1: THE WINTER PARTY

One evening in early December, teachers at Chavez School joined a group of students' parents to plan the Winter Party. The Winter Party was an annual tradition that involved students rotating among the rooms, participating in an activity station led by a parent volunteer. Rather than generating ideas on their own and assigning volunteers, the teachers invited parents to brainstorm potential activities.

As the meeting started, the teachers explained the party format and solicited ideas. One parent recommended a station where students could decorate paper Christmas trees. Another suggested a station where students could pin tails on reindeer, eliciting excited agreement among other attendees. A third parent suggested, "How about a game in which the kids identify the missing words in popular Christmas carols?"

As the meeting progressed, the group started to identify adults willing to lead each station. Ms. Mahdi was happy to volunteer and was asked to lead the Christmas carol game. She agreed, but then added, "I have not been in this country long enough to know the popular songs. I will need a sheet of answers too."

Ms. Mahdi's statement prompted Mr. Olson, whose stepson attended the school, to scan the list of activities more closely. "Wait a minute," he said. "Did anybody notice these are all Christmas activities?" He suggested adding a station related to Hanukkah, such as a dreidel craft. Others nodded in agreement and praised Mr. Olson for making the event more inclusive.

"What about a game or project to represent Kwanzaa?" another parent asked. "I can find something on the Internet."

Hearing this, Ms. Mahdi said, "I thought this was supposed to be a *winter* party, maybe we shouldn't have religious based activities." Several parents opposed this suggestion, explaining that children enjoy Christmas-themed activities.

"These activities aren't *religious*," Ms. Tyler said. "It's really more cultural, more *American* than religious."

Sensing the growing tension, Mr. Olson reminded the group that the Fall Party in October was based mostly on Halloween instead of seasonal activities. "Maybe there's some confusion with the name," he said. "Why don't we call it a *Holiday Party* and celebrate *all* of the holidays?" he asked.

One teacher, Ms. Tate, replied that Chavez's principal suggested at a staff meeting the event should be called a *Winter Party* to be more inclusive. She added, "Honestly, nobody's raised any concerns in the past. Let's just write down all the ideas and then vote?" She began writing a list of suggested activities on the whiteboard.

As she wrote, a parent who had been quiet complained, "I think we are trying too hard to be politically correct. These are *children*. It's no big deal to do some Christmas activities as long as we also have other activities."

Ms. Tate was pleased that family members were taking ownership of the party, but worried that this conversation might alienate some of them. She also noted *most* people at the meeting did not see a problem with the Christmas theme, despite religious diversity at the school.

She wondered whether she should step in and reiterate the spirit of the principal's policy. *Maybe I should be even more direct and* insist *we remove references to religious holidays*, she thought. On the other hand, the last thing she wanted to do was alienate all the people who showed up to plan. She knew she had to do something, though, and soon.

Questions

1 Mr. Olson suggested that they call the event a Holiday Party and try to include "all of the holidays." What do you think he meant by "all of the holidays"? Do you believe his suggestion is a good one? Why or why not?

2 What kind of privilege can happen when teachers and schools turn decision-making over to parents? How can teachers and schools encourage parent engagement and empowerment and ensure that multiple viewpoints are heard?

3 What role can teachers play in either ensuring equity or enshrining privilege in the ways that they communicate with or "hear" from different parents? How can a teacher's biases, perhaps subconscious, impact who is truly "heard"?

CASE 4.2: CHRISTMAS LIGHTS?

While driving home from work later than usual one October evening, Ms. Bren, a teacher at Mendez School, noticed a few houses with lights of various colors strung around their roofs and landscaping. Despite the relatively small number of these houses, Ms. Bren found herself becoming annoyed by the sight of Christmas lights so early in the fall. One house even had a string of lights on the inside of its front window, twinkling brightly. *It's not even Halloween yet!* Ms. Bren thought.

Once home Ms. Bren could not resist sharing what she saw so she sent out a tweet: "Just saw homes w/Christmas lights already! Anyone else as annoyed as I am?!" She felt validated when several friends responded with similar sentiments.

The next day, as students filed into their first period class, Ms. Bren noticed Juan, who always wore a smile, seemed bothered and was unusually quiet. She asked how he was doing. He shrugged as he walked to his seat. *Must have had a bad morning*, Ms. Bren thought.

Moments later her colleague, Mr. Richards, walked into her classroom. "Good morning Ms. Bren," he said. "I saw your tweet yesterday but couldn't respond." He laughed. "I agree! Displaying Christmas lights before Halloween is ridiculous."

Ms. Bren added, "Thank goodness I'm not the only one who feels that way. People are hanging lights earlier every year. Next year we'll start seeing them before Labor Day!"

Mr. Richards continued to chuckle as he left her classroom. Ms. Bren issued her typical morning check-in: "How are you all today?"

She noticed several students, including Juan, looked a little withdrawn. "Did I miss something this morning?" she asked. "Some of you don't seem to be in your typical joyful moods."

"We're cool, Ms. B," responded Hasan, though Ms. Bren noticed he avoided eye contact. He then muttered something about ignorance but because she was not sure what he had heard, Ms. Bren chose to ignore his comment. "All right then," she said with a sigh before adding, "You all can inform me of any problems whenever you're ready, but for now let's have a productive class." She began her lesson.

Later that day Ms. Wilson, one of Ms. Bren's colleagues, dropped by her classroom.

"Do you have a second?" Ms. Wilson asked.

"Sure," Ms. Bren replied. "What's up?"

"Well," Ms. Wilson said, "I wanted to let you know I overheard Hasan and several other students talking about a tweet you sent last night. Something about Christmas lights. They seemed upset and said you and Mr. Richards had no business insulting their friend's family."

Ms. Bren felt sick to her stomach. "Thanks for letting me know," she replied, embarrassed by what she had just learned. As Ms. Wilson walked out of the room, Ms. Bren wondered how her students knew about her tweet and who else she might have offended. She also wondered if this explained why some students seemed disengaged during her class.

Questions

1 What assumptions, if any, did Ms. Bren make as she was driving through the neighborhood close to her school? Why might she be inclined to make these assumptions?

2 What impact might the conversation between Ms. Bren and Mr. Richards have had for the students who were listening and whose families did have lights on their houses? What impact might it have had for students who were listening but who did not have lights on their houses?

3 Should Ms. Bren censor what she communicates through social media because she is a teacher?

CASE 4.3: A DIFFERENCE IN PERSPECTIVES

Upon entering his classroom, Mr. Ortiz noticed several students crowded around two of their peers, Nikhil and Jasper. They were arguing about something Nikhil was wearing.

Mr. Ortiz asked the students to take their seats and inquired about the conflict. Jasper explained, "Nikhil is wearing a swastika. It's offensive." Mr. Ortiz glanced at Nikhil but didn't notice anything controversial about his attire. Before he could inquire further, Nikhil looked at Jasper and retorted, "You're ignorant!? My grandmother gave this to me."

"Whoa!" Mr. Ortiz replied. "Perhaps someone other than Jasper or Nikhil can explain what's going on." Madelyn shared, "Nikhil is wearing a gold chain and swastika pendant from his grandmother. Jasper got upset and asked Nikhil why he was wearing a Nazi symbol. Nikhil said it's an ancient Hindu symbol, but Jasper cut him off and said that it shouldn't be allowed in school because it represents hate." She continued, "I agree with Jasper. It's not cool for Nikhil to wear it."

"May I see your necklace, Nikhil?" Mr. Ortiz asked. Nikhil pulled the gold chain out from under his t-shirt, revealing a pendant that looked like a swastika.

"That was a gift from your grandmother?" asked Mr. Ortiz.

"Yeah," replied Nikhil. "She passed away. I'm wearing it to honor her."

"You understand this symbol is offensive to a lot of people, right?" Mr. Ortiz asked.

"Yes, but it's *not* the Nazi symbol. If people learn the history, they'll see it's no different from wearing a cross pendant." Several students quickly expressed disagreement.

"OK, OK," said Mr. Ortiz. "Quiet down. This is a longer discussion than we have time for right now. We'll discuss it later, I assure you."

"That's fine with me," responded Jasper. "But Nikhil should take it off until then." As Mr. Ortiz was thinking about what to say, he saw Madelyn waving her hand, eager to share something.

"Yes, Madelyn?" he asked.

"Nikhil is telling the truth," Madelyn shared. "I looked it up and that *is* an ancient Hindu symbol. It's been used in other religions before it became a Nazi symbol."

"*Of course* I'm telling the truth," Nikhil responded. "This chain means a lot to me and I'm not taking it off just because people are ignorant."

Mr. Ortiz didn't know anything about the history of the symbol, but he knew Nikhil's pendant could be disruptive to some students. Although learning more about it would be a great educational opportunity, he worried it would be impossible for the conversation to reach everyone and did not want to deal with additional disruptions. He proposed a solution to Nikhil.

"You are right about our ignorance, Nikhil," he said, "but your necklace is causing a disruption, since most people think it is symbol of hate. Perhaps you can honor your grandmother by wearing it at home."

"No," responded Nikhil, "It's not fair other students can display religious symbols and I can't. I'm not taking it off."

Mr. Ortiz sighed, "OK, but keep it under your shirt."

Once class finished and the students headed to lunch, Mr. Ortiz knew it would be only a matter of time before others learned about Nikhil's pendant. *We need to figure this out quickly*, he thought.

Questions

1 Nikhil believes it is unjust to allow other students to display religious symbols while he is not allowed to do the same. Do you agree? Why or why not?
2 It appears as though Mr. Ortiz is concerned about the lack of time he has to address the issue in class. If you were Mr. Ortiz, how would you address the situation given the time limitations?
3 Should Mr. Ortiz and other educators at the school educate the student body about the history of this religious symbol so that Nikhil can continue wearing the necklace? How might the religious identities of people in the school and broader community influence your response?

CASE 4.4: ISLAMOPHOBIC READ-ALOUD

Ms. McGrath, a language arts and journalism teacher at Grove School, was determined to help students learn how to write thoughtfully about complex social issues. She raised a few eyebrows for encouraging students to write about everything from oil pipelines to gun control. However, she always was determined to keep her views on these issues to herself, so although her teaching elicited an occasional complaint, her principal was supportive and the tension always waned quickly.

Ms. McGrath also believed students interested in journalism needed to stay apprised of current events. She started every class with a question: "What's new today?"

Grove was populated predominantly by Christian and upper middle-class students. It was located near Washington, D.C. A small but growing population of Muslim students, mostly children of diplomats from upper middle-class families, recently started attending the school. Ms. McGrath knew some of the Muslim students had experienced bullying, but for the most part, from what she could see in her classes, everybody got along well.

A couple weeks into the new school year, with the anniversary of the September 11, 2001, attacks on the World Trade Center and Pentagon approaching, her students began talking about news stories commemorating the event. Sensitive to the likelihood that some students' families had been impacted directly by the attacks given the school's proximity to the Pentagon, Ms. McGrath developed a writing activity on the topic.

A few days before the anniversary, Ms. McGrath asked students to do a free write, reminding them to write whatever comes to mind. Then she gave them a prompt: "What, in your opinion, has been the impact of the events of September 11, 2001, on the United States?" She gave students five minutes to write.

After the five minutes Ms. McGrath asked for volunteers to read their free writes to the class. George, an outspoken student known for frequently referencing his Christian faith in classes, was the only student volunteering. She reluctantly looked at him and nodded, and he stood to read his free write.

"I believe most people are good," he read, "but I believe 9/11 was a tragedy brought to this country by an immoral religion, and we continue to see more terrorist attacks because of this religion. That is why we need to ban more Muslims from entering our country."

Ms. McGrath considered interrupting George at this point, but remembered that when they first shared their free writes, she set the ground rule, *we listen carefully and mindfully, without interrupting*. She felt stuck.

George continued, "But what's most important is that the attacks helped us remember how important it is that we Christians need to protect American values."

George bowed playfully and sat down. Ms. McGrath, scanning the room, saw several students nodding. Hasina, a Muslim student, stared down at her desk. Essam, another Muslim student, looked at Ms. McGrath as if to say, "Are you going to respond to that?"

Ms. McGrath knew she needed to respond, but she was not sure how.

Questions

1   Should Ms. McGrath have interrupted George's reading despite her own ground rule? Why or why not? If she had decided to interrupt his reading, how might she have addressed George's anti-Muslim sentiments?

2   Ms. McGrath had developed a reputation for being balanced on controversial issues, which is part of what allowed her to continue to engage students around those issues despite the occasional complaint. What was her responsibility in this scenario? Should she have taken a stand against George's views? Why or why not?

3   What are the implications of how Ms. McGrath responded when it comes to Hasina and Essam? What are the implications for the other students?

5

CASES ON ETHNICITY AND CULTURE

CASE 5.1: PROTESTING THE PLEDGE

As they filed into his classroom, Mr. Harrold overheard students discussing the score of a professional football game from the previous evening. When the conversation subsided, one student, Caylee, mentioned a player on the losing team who refused to stand during the national anthem. "Losing is karma for not respecting the American flag," she proclaimed. A few of her classmates laughed and nodded in agreement. Another student added, "His team probably lost because of the distraction."

"Oh boy," Mr. Harrold thought. "Is this something I need to address?" His mind turned to all the content he needed to cover and his carefully planned lesson, so he decided not to respond to Caylee's comment.

Later that evening as he watched the news Mr. Harrold saw highlights from the football game the students had discussed. The reporter addressed the backlash the player received for not standing during the national anthem. She interviewed both people who supported the player's decision and others who opposed it. Mr. Harrold wondered about his decision not to address Caylee's comment but felt the teachable moment had passed.

Several weeks later Mr. Harrold overheard students talking about a classmate who had chosen earlier in the day not to stand during the Pledge of Allegiance. When asked by classmates about her decision, Kate had explained, "I don't believe 'liberty and justice for all' exist in our country."

A couple of her classmates expressed disdain for her behavior. They said Kate was only protesting because she wanted attention, not because of her cultural or political beliefs.

Once again Mr. Harrold was unsure how to respond. He knew this was a sensitive topic eliciting heated debates among adults, so he knew he needed to proceed with caution. He also knew his school prided itself on the annual Veterans Day program and wondered whether promoting dialogue about sitting during the national anthem or Pledge of Allegiance would be seen by some people in the community as conflicting with the school's history of honoring military veterans.

As he lost himself in reflection about how or whether to address the situation, a student interrupted his contemplation. "Mr. Harrold," the student asked, "do you think it's disrespectful to not stand during the Pledge or national anthem? Isn't it a school rule that we have to stand?"

Questions

1 How, if at all, should Mr. Harrold's personal opinion about protesting the national anthem or Pledge of Allegiance inform how he responds to the student's question at the end of the case?

2 Should teachers address social or political issues mentioned during casual conversations by students? Should they address these issues even if doing so cuts into instructional time for the planned lesson?

3 One of Kate's reasons for not standing during the Pledge was that she didn't feel the words accurately represented everyone's reality. What are other reasons people might feel compelled to not stand during the national anthem or Pledge of Allegiance?

CASE 5.2: NOT TIME FOR STORIES

Ms. Ward loved geography. She inspired and motivated students by telling them they were learning material typically reserved for older students.

The first unit Ms. Ward planned for the new school year focused on California. Although Rustin School, where Ms. Ward taught, was in the Midwest, she thought it would be a fun state with which to kick off the year. Students at Rustin represented a wide range of socioeconomic and racial diversity, but she knew many of them were interested in ocean beaches. California, in her mind, fit well with this theme.

Ms. Ward gathered her students on the carpet and began writing on a flip chart. Several students whispered excitedly as she wrote "California" at the top of the sheet. Although Ms. Ward was happy to see their excitement, she reminded them to remain quiet and raise their hands if they had something to say. Immediately several hands flew up.

"Are we going to learn about California?" Maddy asked.

"Yes," Ms. Ward replied. "We will be learning about California in many of our subjects throughout the week." Students chattered excitedly again and Ms. Ward reminded them to remain quiet: "I cannot understand you if so many of you talk at once."

After explaining the unit a bit more, Ms. Ward asked who had been to California. DeQuan raised his hand. When Ms. Ward called on him he said, "A few days ago, I was at my grandmother's house watching television with my little sister, but she was crying so I couldn't hear very well. I told her to be quiet and gave her a toy to play with because the person on TV..."

Ms. Ward interrupted DeQuan and reminded him that the question she asked was who had been to California. Growing bothered by the side chatter and DeQuan's indirect answer, she reminded the class that now was not the time for stories.

"Please raise your hand *only* if you can answer the question," she said. Upon hearing this, DeQuan angrily added, "I was saying that the person on TV said the show was sponsored by a company that makes raisins, which are my favorite snack, and that the raisins are made in California!"

Ms. Ward reminded DeQuan he needed to raise his hand if he had something to say, and added that his tone was disrespectful. Attempting to refocus the group, she asked, "Has anyone been to Disneyland?" Maddy raised her hand and said, "I have. It's in California, and it is sunny and warm there. It's also far away because we were on the airplane for a long time."

"You're right," Ms. Ward replied as she wrote "warm" and "sunny" along with the phrase "far from Rustin School" on the flip chart.

"Any other words to describe California?" she asked. As several others raised their hands, Ms. Ward noticed DeQuan still looked angry. Anticipating another outburst, she cheerfully said, "DeQuan, please try to compose yourself so that you can remain seated with the group." Hearing this, DeQuan stood, walked to his desk, and slouched in his chair.

Oh no, thought Ms. Ward. *He must not have heard me correctly.* Knowing time was passing quickly and that she needed to finish the lesson, Ms. Ward continued teaching but wondered how she should address DeQuan if his negative behavior persisted.

Questions

1 How did Ms. Ward's behavior in this scenario fail to ensure an equitable and just learning environment for all her students?
2 What differences can you identify in Maddy's and DeQuan's responses to their teacher's question? What similarities can you identify?
3 In anticipation of another "outburst," Ms. Ward gave DeQuan some instructions. What might have caused DeQuan to react the way he did? What long-term effects can result if Ms. Ward does not remedy the situation?

CASE 5.3: TEACHING THANKSGIVING

Ms. Porter raised her hand nervously. It was the beginning of her school's staff meeting and her principal, Ms. Chang, had asked if anybody wanted to add new items to the agenda. "I'd like to talk about how we plan to teach about the upcoming Thanksgiving holiday," Ms. Porter said.

Several colleagues responded.

"I don't plan to talk about it at all. Thanksgiving seems to be more about consumerism than spending time with family," Mr. Espinosa said.

Ms. Tilson commented, "I focus on food. Students are really engaged when we talk about food. We'll talk about how the Pilgrims and

Indians shared a feast, and since some of our students are immigrants, we can use it as an opportunity to learn about traditional foods."

"I focus on the Thanks in Thanksgiving," Mr. Webster added. "We all have so much to be thankful for. I like to focus on the positive."

Ms. Chang replied, "Seems we have a variety of ways to honor the holiday. I don't think we need any more conversation on this unless you have questions."

Ms. Porter's mind was most concerned with what her colleagues were not intending to talk about. She anxiously wondered how she could emphasize the importance of discussing American Indian perspectives with students without offending her colleagues. "Well," she said, "I'm concerned with how we are perpetuating myths about the first Thanksgiving. I'm concerned we are not acknowledging that some Indigenous people observe this day as a day of mourning, not as a celebration. This is a great opportunity to promote dialogue within the school community about popular customs that might alienate some students and families, such as pretending to be Pilgrims and Indians."

As she heard these words coming out of her mouth, Ms. Porter felt a wave of relief and regret. She was bothered by the way many of her colleagues had addressed Thanksgiving in previous years but never felt comfortable speaking up.

"We have so many needs in our school. I don't think we should micromanage how people teach Thanksgiving. We don't even have any of those students in our school," Ms. Tilson said.

Ms. Chang, sensing tension in the room, replied, "You all have great points. Thank you for sharing them. It seems this is a larger topic than we have time to discuss now. Maybe those of you who are interested in exploring it further can create a presentation for one of our professional development days in the spring." With that comment, she moved to the next item on the agenda.

Ms. Porter looked around the room, frustrated by her colleagues' comments, and that nobody else spoke up or supported her for speaking up. She knew everyone felt overwhelmed with work as holiday breaks. She doubted anyone would volunteer to develop a presentation after the holidays passed.

"There goes another year," she thought to herself.

Questions

1 Which character in this scenario most resonates with you? Why?
2 Do teachers have an obligation to incorporate multiple perspectives when discussing holidays? Is this dependent on which identity groups are represented in the student population?
3 How should this situation be addressed before another Thanksgiving passes?

CASE 5.4: MULTICULTURAL DAY PARADE

In an effort to celebrate the growing racial and ethnic diversity at Eastern School, the school's Diversity Committee decided to sponsor Multicultural Day. Numerous performers were hired for assemblies and presentations. During the day's feature event, the "Culture Parade," students were asked to showcase cultural clothing as they walked through the hallways. Teachers were encouraged by the committee to discuss clothing from countries outside the United States and to invite students who had such clothing to bring it to school for the parade.

Ms. Morrison was excited about Multicultural Day because many of her students had parents who were immigrants. She imagined the day as an opportunity for those students to teach others about their cultures.

A week before the event, Ms. Morrison brought a kilt to class and explained its significance to the students. "This represents my Scottish heritage," she said, "and I am proud to show it to you today." She then asked whether students had "special costumes" at home that represented their cultures. Several students raised their hands, which prompted Ms. Morrison to discuss the events planned for Multicultural Day, including the parade.

During dismissal the day before the parade Ms. Morrison announced, "Don't forget to bring your costumes to class tomorrow!"

The next day, Ms. Morrison was pleased to see several Hmong and Liberian students came with bags of clothing. She saw that two other students, Emily and Keisha, brought clothing, so she inquired about what was in their bags. Emily, a white student, excitedly pulled out her soccer uniform, and Keisha, an African American student, pulled jeans and her favorite sweatshirt out of her bag. Ms. Morrison told the two girls she appreciated their enthusiasm for Multicultural Day but that they would not be able to walk in the parade. She explained that what Keisha and Emily brought was everyday clothing rather than clothes that represented their ethnic heritages.

Both girls protested. "This outfit represents my culture," Keisha argued.

Ms. Morrison shared with the girls that she felt terrible about the confusion, but could not allow them to participate. "Maybe next year they'll expand the parade," she said.

After the girls walked away, Ms. Morrison considered changing her mind. She worried, though, that other students or staff would be puzzled by their participation and that Keisha and Emily would be ridiculed for not following directions.

Questions

1 What images come to mind when you hear the term "costume"? In what ways might it be considered demeaning?
2 Often people conflate "culture," "ethnicity," "heritage," "race," and "nationality," or use them interchangeably. How are these concepts different from one another? Is a "Multicultural Day" different than an "International Day"?
3 How might activities that require students to share part of their ethnic heritage alienate students or contribute to students' and teachers' existing stereotypes and biases?

CASE 5.5: A PLACE TO STUDY

It was Back to School Night. Ms. Grady decided over summer she wanted to cultivate better at-home study habits in students. Many families came to Ms. Grady's classroom that night and listened as she explained how important it was for students to have a designated place at home to study and keep learning materials.

In order to motivate students, Ms. Grady purchased a pencil box for each of them to take home. She filled the boxes with writing instruments. Shua, one of Ms. Grady's students, was especially excited about the pencil box. Ms. Grady was excited for Shua because at the Back to School event, his parents seemed responsive to her suggestions.

A month into the school year, Ms. Grady noticed Shua was turning in homework with food stains. She also noticed he was crossing out some answers instead of erasing them. When she asked Shua about this he explained his siblings also had been using his pencils and pens. They did not always return them, which was why he had not been using an eraser.

"And the food stains?" Ms. Grady asked. Shua explained he and his older brother do homework at the kitchen table, sometimes while others were eating.

Ms. Grady was sympathetic to Shua's situation and decided to give him another set of utensils, which she labeled with his name. "Remember to find a quiet, *separate* place to work instead of working and keeping your box of utensils at the table," she told him. Shua nodded.

A few weeks later, after seeing little change in the condition of Shua's homework, Ms. Grady followed up with him regarding where he was studying and whether his siblings were still using his utensils. Noticeably uncomfortable, Shua replied, "I still work at the table and sometimes they still use my stuff." Ms. Grady thanked Shua for his honesty.

Later, when the school day ended, she wondered how she should approach Shua's parents at the upcoming parent-teacher conferences. She remembered they seemed supportive about her expectations that students have a quiet place to study. If they were supportive in front of her, but did not follow through at home, she worried they also would not be supportive of her other ideas for at-home learning. She also wondered whether Shua's family might benefit from a referral to a local agency that could provide donations if the family needed school supplies or other household items, since his siblings were using Shua's supplies.

Feeling frustrated, she packed her things and left for the day.

Questions

1 What outcome was Ms. Grady hoping to achieve by talking about study habits during the Back to School meeting? Do you feel her strategies were useful? Why or why not?

2 Was Ms. Grady's expectation for how the pencil case should be used reasonable, especially considering she gave him more than one? Why or why not?

3 How might Ms. Grady's frustrations impact her interaction with Shua and his family during the upcoming conference or for the remainder of the school year?

6

CASES ON RACE

CASE 6.1: BLACK LIVES MATTER

It was a Friday afternoon. Ms. Simmons, a teacher at East City School, wondered how the protest was shaping up. Local Black Lives Matter (BLM) activists had organized a protest just a few blocks from the school. They had done all the proper paperwork to site their protest in the area. Still, because the protest was scheduled for the block of time between when schools let out and when rush hour ends, Ms. Simmons knew tensions would be high.

If the mood of the adults who came by East City to pick up their children was any indication, her concerns were warranted. When she left school around 4:30 p.m., traffic was still a mess. She noticed several school buses trapped in the gridlock. Although she found an alternate route and got home just a half hour later than usual, the buses weren't as easily navigated through intersections full of pedestrians and protesters.

Having been an activist herself, Ms. Simmons understood protests could be disruptive. She was proud of the protesters for raising awareness about racism and demanding accountability in light of the recent spate of police shootings of unarmed African American men. These included one incident just a couple towns over from East City. For Ms. Simmons, the inconvenience posed by a blocked road was well worth the message being spread by the protesters.

Unfortunately, many adults trying to get to the school to pick up their children or waiting for their children at home were not as forgiving. They were frustrated with the protestors and angry the city allowed them to protest at a busy intersection near the school. Local news outlets covered the protest's traffic disturbance and parent frustrations about the traffic as heavily as the protest itself. Parents complained about BLM's "divisiveness" and circulated their complaints on social media.

Monday morning Ms. Simmons noticed a few students wearing t-shirts with the words "All Lives Matter" and a few wearing shirts with the words "Black Lives Matter." She could feel the tension. She saw an opportunity to engage students in a conversation about the protest and racism in the local community, but when she mentioned her desire to raise these issues in class to colleagues, they discouraged her. "Stick to academics," one colleague said.

With the first period bell set to ring, Ms. Simmons decided to ignore her colleagues' advice and hoped her teaching instincts would be sufficient to make the conversation constructive and informative. She wondered what she should say first.

Questions

1 What are some reasons educators might be fearful about introducing conversations about racism in their classes? What can school leaders do to alleviate that fear? What can we do as individual educators to alleviate that fear in ourselves?

2 If you were a teacher at East City, how would you respond to students wearing "All Lives Matter" shirts to help them distinguish that point from the importance of a movement insisting "Black Lives Matter"?

3 If you were Ms. Simmons, what pedagogical strategies would you use to engage students in a conversation about racism and the BLM movement? Are there issues or topics about which you feel you would need to learn more before doing this?

CASE 6.2: TEACHING RACE WITH *HUCKLEBERRY FINN*

Samuel, one of three African American students in Ms. Kohl's language arts class, loved discussing literature. Ms. Kohl loved having students act out the stories they read to connect more deeply with characters. Samuel always volunteered to play one of the characters.

Ms. Kohl's favorite novel was Mark Twain's *The Adventures of Huckleberry Finn*. When her students returned to class after reading its first fifty pages, she couldn't wait to begin the reenactment.

She was aware, of course, that this approach was risky with *Huck Finn*, which was full of racialized language. She considered talking with students about the use of the n-word in the novel before they read it. But she resisted, concerned that such a discussion might manipulate students into a particular view of the book.

Once students were settled into their desks, she asked for volunteers: "Who wants to play a role?" Several students raised their hands but, to Ms. Kohl's surprise, Samuel was not one of them. In fact, he appeared distracted. As classmates moved to the front of the room to play a role, he stared down at his desk.

"How about you, Samuel?" Ms. Kohl asked. "Didn't you like the novel?"

"It was all right," he answered.

"Well everyone can't love every piece of literature," she said, continuing with the lesson.

Johnny, one of Samuel's white classmates, volunteered to play the role of Huck, which also made him the narrator of the story. He played his role with verve, trying his best to sound the way he imagined Huck sounding.

Initially Samuel sat quietly, following the story in his book. But within minutes Ms. Kohl noticed him growing listless, shifting in his seat.

"Everything OK, Samuel?" she asked.

"Not really," he answered.

"What's going on?"

"I hate this book."

"Yes, well, everyone can't love every piece of literature," Ms. Kohl said again. "Let's get through these first ten pages. Then I'd like to hear why you don't like it."

Samuel sighed.

Samuel's classmates continued to read. Ms. Kohl, noticing that Samuel remained uncomfortable, started to worry it might be because of the racialized language.

The students had reached the eighth page of the novel. Ms. Kohl always felt nervous about page eight because, although the n-word was scattered through the first seven pages, it appeared several times on page eight. Ms. Kohl's thoughts were interrupted by the sound of Samuel shouting, "Stop it! You think saying that is OK? Shut up!"

Samuel threw his book on the floor and exited loudly out of the room, slamming the door behind him. Ms. Kohl, looking up to find twenty-six students as shocked as she was, had no idea what to do next.

Questions

1 How might Ms. Kohl have prepared her students for the language in *Huck Finn*? Should she have done so before they began reading the novel, or do you agree with her not wanting to "spoil" their experience of the book by talking too much about it before reading it?

2 Should teachers assign readings that use the n-word or other oppressive language? Some people argue that such language should be removed from literature used in schools. Do you agree? Why or why not?

3 Should Samuel be punished for his outburst and for walking out of the classroom the same way another student would have been punished if it had happened on another day for another reason? How might Ms. Kohl address the situation with her other students?

CASE 6.3: DIVERSE FRIENDS DAY

When Mr. Carbondale started teaching at Lozen School more than twenty years ago, the students, like the teachers and administrators, were almost all white. This began to change ten years ago when gentrification started driving more families of color out of the city to seek affordable housing. Now more than 40 percent of the student body was comprised of students of color. Mr. Carbondale was happy to see the racial demographics of the student body changing.

Mr. Carbondale often volunteered to represent his school at the day-long "Inclusive Excellence" conference hosted each year by his district. At the most recent of these conferences, he found one idea most intriguing: Diverse Friends Day. Students were encouraged to spend one day interacting with classmates with whom they normally wouldn't interact. They would eat lunch at a new table, sit by different people during class, and challenge themselves to shake up their social groups in other ways. The goal was to encourage greater intergroup interaction, especially across race.

The following Monday Mr. Carbondale secured permission from his principal to organize Diverse Friends Day. A day was selected just one month away.

Mr. Carbondale couldn't wait to share the news about the event with his students. Having just read a series of Langston Hughes poems, they had spent several class periods in spirited discussions about race relations. He expected some resistance. These were young people, after all, whose identities were influenced mostly by their social groups. But they also were curious about social groups to which they did not belong. Mr. Carbondale hoped this curiosity would override their anxieties about stepping out of their comfort zones.

As he had guessed, when Mr. Carbondale told students about Diverse Friends Day, a few protested, while others seemed excited. He noted, though, that Pam and Tariq, the two African American students in his class, and Julio, one of three Mexican American students in his class, remained silent. Not wanting to put them on the spot, he decided to reach out to them after class.

Once class ended, Mr. Carbondale pulled them aside and asked their thoughts on Diverse Friends Day. "I know you mean well, but that program is racist," Pam shared.

Shocked, Mr. Carbondale asked her to elaborate.

"I don't know about 'racist,'" Tariq interjected, "but I don't want to do it."

"I think it sounds kind of fun," Julio said, "but a lot of the white people in this school don't like us and call us names. I don't want to be forced to hang out with people who do that."

"Why do you think it's racist?" Mr. Carbondale asked Pam, noticing the tension on her face.

"There's a lot of racism in this school. Lunch is the only time I can relax, when I can be with my friends. I think Diverse Friends Day is for white people."

Unsettled and unsure what to say next, Mr. Carbondale thanked the students for their honesty. As they left he added, "I promise I'll think about what you shared."

Questions

1 What do you think Pam meant when she said, "I think Diverse Friends Day is for white people"? Can you think of other "diversity" programs in schools that might elicit similar reactions from some students of color?

2 How might Lozen School address the institutional culture of the school, as well as the racial inequities being experienced by students, rather than focusing just on race relations and celebrating diversity?

3 Pam told Mr. Carbondale that lunch is the only time during school when she can relax without feeling judged. Other than students of color, what sorts of students might share that experience with Pam?

CASE 6.4: TERMS OF ENDEARMENT

Ms. Lawson, a teacher at Audre Lorde School, previously worked at predominantly white and wealthier schools. This year, however, she was excited to accept a job in a more racially and economically diverse environment.

Several weeks into her first year at the new school, Ms. Lawson reflected on her adjustment. She had taken several measures to demonstrate her commitment to racial equity and it seemed students were responding positively. She was especially pleased when she saw students of color reading the Diversity in Mathematics posters she hung around the room, highlighting historically important mathematicians of color.

One afternoon, as students made their way into her classroom, Ms. Lawson overhead one student use the n-word. Understanding how inflammatory the n-word was, her immediate concern was that there would be a fight in her classroom. So when she looked up from her computer and peered toward the back of her classroom, from where she was sure the word came, she was surprised to see Reggie, an African American student and Anthony, a white student, laughing together.

"Who said that?" Ms. Lawson asked as she walked toward the back of the room.

"Said what?" Anthony asked, still laughing.

"The n-word," Ms. Lawson replied. Nobody responded, but Reggie glanced at Anthony.

"Anthony?" Ms. Lawson prodded.

"I didn't say the n-word, I said *n–i–g–g–a, nigga*," he explained. "I call Reggie that and he's cool with it because we're friends. It's a term of endearment."

Keisha, an African American young woman who had overheard their conversation, interjected, "That's not a term of endearment, you idiot. It's racist. You're lucky you're not getting a beat down for saying it."

"No threats," Ms. Lawson said, glaring at Keisha. "Let me take care of this."

Unsure what to say next, Ms. Lawson turned toward Reggie. He looked uncomfortable. "Is that true, Reggie, that you're fine with it?"

"It's no big deal," Anthony explained playfully.

"Reggie can speak for himself," Ms. Lawson said, then looked back at Reggie, looking even more uncomfortable. Just then, the start of class bell rang and Ms. Lawson noticed everybody staring at Reggie. Sensing that whatever he really felt about Anthony's use of the n-word, Reggie was even more uneasy with the spotlight she was shining on him, so she decided to drop the issue and begin class.

As she walked back toward her desk, Ms. Lawson said with a half-defeated sigh, "Please remember one of our community norms is *respect*. I don't care how you pronounce it, there is no room for that kind of language."

She felt, even as she was making this statement, that she did not handle the situation well.

Questions

1 Is there any circumstance in which it would be fine for somebody to use the n-word or any variation of it in a classroom or school? If so, what would that circumstance be?

2 How could Ms. Lawson have addressed Keisha's comments more effectively, instead of chastising her out of fear of escalating tensions?

3 What are other ways Ms. Lawson might have checked in with Reggie to avoid shining the spotlight on him? How might she use the teachable moment to address the use of the n-word with her entire class.

CASE 6.5: AN UNCOMFORTABLE FIELD TRIP

It was field trip day and Ms. Anderson, a teacher at Boggs School, was excited. She had sent a letter asking for a representative of a renowned advertising agency to visit one of her classes during a marketing unit and was thrilled when the agency suggested, instead, that her class should visit the agency for a tour. The day would be filled with opportunities for students to learn about careers in marketing. They would even be treated to a catered lunch. Ms. Anderson hoped the trip would inspire the students, many of whom would be first generation college students and had limited exposure to the business world.

The day before the field trip Ms. Anderson reminded the students to dress more formally than they usually dressed for school. However, as she watched students trickle into class on field trip day, she noticed two students of color, Hakeem and Kevin, wearing sneakers with their dress pants. Not wanting to embarrass them, she approached them and jokingly said, "I guess your shoes will come in handy if we play basketball during the visit." Both students smiled as they sat down. Ms. Anderson discussed behavior expectations for the day.

Later, when students arrived at the agency, a company representative greeted them and started the tour. As they walked through one of the workspaces, the tour leader mentioned that many of the employees were hired directly out of college and that many had attended prestigious colleges in the country. "If you have excellent grades and work hard, you also could work here," she said. "And once you're in we take good care of you."

Ms. Anderson noticed Hakeem and Kevin looking at each other and rolling their eyes in response to the tour guide's comment.

Then she saw Kevin whisper something to Hakeem, at which they both laughed. Ms. Anderson discreetly reminded them to be respectful.

As the tour continued, she saw Hakeem smirk in response to a comment made by one of the agency executives. Feeling frustrated and embarrassed, Ms. Anderson pulled him aside and told him how generous the ad agency was to invite the students on this tour. "We should be appreciative, not disrespectful," she chided. "If this continues, you'll have to wait in the lobby and miss the rest of the activities." Hakeem and Kevin remained quiet during the rest of the tour, but appeared disengaged.

Once they returned to school, Ms. Anderson asked the class to share what they enjoyed most about the trip. A few students mentioned how fun it was to be downtown and to visit such a cool office. Others talked about still feeling hungry after their "fancy lunch."

When Ms. Anderson asked whether they would want to work at the agency, Kevin responded with a grin, "It seems like *you* want to work there." Several students laughed. Kevin continued, "It was good not having to be at school, though."

Really? Ms. Anderson thought to herself once the students left. *I guess I took the wrong group of students.* She wondered what she could have done differently to make the day more successful.

Questions

1 Was Ms. Anderson's attempt to connect with Hakeem and Kevin and inquire about their shoes appropriate? Why might the boys have been wearing sneakers with their dress pants?

2 Why might some of Ms. Anderson's students have been uncomfortable at the ad agency? What might have kept some of them from just letting Ms. Anderson know they were uncomfortable?

3 In what ways, if at all, should Ms. Anderson have prepared students for this field trip? In what ways could she have prepared the ad agency to mindfully host her students?

CASE 6.6: BUILD THE WALL

Mr. Bertrand, the men's basketball coach at Westfield, a school attended predominantly by Latinx and Cherokee students, had been warned by other area coaches that the student section at the predominantly white Green Hills School could be ruthless in their treatment of visiting teams. Despite Green Hills being on his team's schedule, he was not concerned. His teams had been ribbed by opposing fans before.

When his team arrived at Green Hills for their game, Mr. Bertrand was surprised by the size of the assembling crowd. He reminded his team, the demographics of which were representative of Westfield's overall student population, not to respond to spectators' comments.

The home team bleachers were full when the game started. Mr. Bertrand noticed an inordinate number of fans wearing American flag shirts and caps, but didn't think much of it. When the first half passed without incident, he assumed the warnings about Green Hills students were overstated.

About halfway through the second half Francisco, Westfield's star player, fouled one of Green Hills' players, inadvertently knocking him down. The Green Hills player stood and shoved Francisco. Francisco did not respond at first, but when the opposing player shoved him again, Francisco shoved him back. Finally, one of the referees wedged himself between the players. The teams briefly jawed at one another.

Trying to defuse the situation, Mr. Bertrand called a timeout. As he waved his team to the bench he heard a faint chant coming from the bleachers. Then it grew louder. Harkening to President Trump's campaign promise to build a border wall between the U.S. and Mexico, fans chanted, "Build-the-wall! Build-the-wall! Build-the-wall!"

Mr. Bertrand felt furious, both because of the racism and xenophobia underlying the chant and because no adult from Green Hills addressed the chant adequately. He looked at the Green Hills coach, who shrugged. He noticed some Green Hills players were laughing while others appeared embarrassed. He scanned the eyes of his players and saw anger, confusion, and sadness. Then he scanned the crowd, noting all the chanters appeared to be students. He finally saw a couple adults imploring the chanting students to stop, and eventually the chant waned.

Mr. Bertrand hoped somebody from Green Hills would be more forceful about addressing the chanters. He also hoped he had the skills to address this situation with his players after the game. But in 90 seconds the referee would blow the whistle to resume play. *What is the right way to handle this right now?* he wondered.

Questions

1 If you were Mr. Bertrand, what would you say to your team? Should Mr. Bertrand find a way during the short time before the game resumes to engage the players in a process of deciding how to respond? If so, how?

2 If you were an educator in the stands, what would you have done? Do educators have an obligation to address after-school behaviors such as this one in their classroom?

3 Should the Green Hills students be educated, punished, or both? On what do they need to be educated? What would be a suitable punishment?

7

CASES ON SEX, GENDER IDENTITY, AND GENDER EXPRESSION

CASE 7.1: BOYS VS. GIRLS TRIVIA CONTEST

Matt, a first-year teacher, walked into Bill's classroom, excited to observe him. Matt had a lot of respect for Bill as a teacher and looked forward to seeing effective classroom management techniques in action. Bill, a teaching veteran, was well liked by students and colleagues. Their principal had recommended that Matt observe Bill, noting how he engaged students, a key to limiting disciplinary interruptions. Matt found a desk in the back of the room and prepared to take notes.

As students settled into their seats, Bill welcomed them cheerily. He then reminded them that one of their benchmark tests was scheduled for the next day. Following a brief overview of strategies for studying the material, Bill asked whether they wanted to play a game. "Let's see how prepared you are for the exam."

"First, we need to split ourselves into two teams," Bill explained, then asked students how they wanted to do so. As students discussed options, Bill walked to the back of the room and said to Matt, "If you let students make decisions, they'll take ownership of their learning."

One student suggested they form teams by gender, "boys versus girls," eliciting enthusiastic support from several classmates. Bill sent the young men to one side of the room and the young women to the other side of room, then proceeded to ask each team questions while keeping count of correct responses.

After ten minutes the "girls" team was well ahead of the "boys" team, leading a couple young men to joke they were "letting the girls win."

A couple young women responded by reminding their male classmates that the "girls" won the previous two games, as well. Following several minutes of the teams mocking one another, Bill tried to refocus all the students by announcing, "If you guys don't settle down we'll end the game."

After class, as students left the room, Matt heard several laughing and making disparaging remarks to one another, debating about which gender was most intelligent. Bill approached Matt and warmly said, "The students love competitions and don't realize how much they're learning in the process."

He then looked down and, seeing Matt's notes, noticed he had written and circled "gender stereotypes" in his notebook. "Whoa! *That's* what you are focusing on?" Bill asked. "Boys versus girls: that's what the students love to do." He then counseled Matt, "You're still new at this and will learn soon enough that, as long as the students are engaged and learning, that other stuff doesn't matter."

With that, Bill walked back to his desk as Matt sat speechless, wondering whether he had been too sensitive.

Questions

1 What are some of the dynamics Matt observed that might have raised concerns about gender stereotypes for him? Is his assessment of "gender stereotypes" justified? Why or why not?

2 What implications about gender might arise for the students in this class? How might students who are transgender or who do not identify with any specific gender group feel as they watch their peers enthusiastically endorse the "boys versus girls" activity?

3 Should educators promote equitable environments even if student demographics might not require it? For example, not allowing "boys versus girls" if there are no students who identify as transgender?

CASE 7.2: GENDERED BATHROOMS

Teryn and her parents had been pleasantly surprised by the support they felt from many of her classmates and teachers at Riverway High School. Teryn faced instances of transphobia and bullying, which escalated when she requested people start calling her Teryn instead of her previous name, David. However, she was appreciative of how the school dealt with these instances, as painful as they were.

Teryn's homeroom teacher, Ms. Harris, tried especially hard to be supportive. For example, on the first day of class she asked students to introduce themselves and share their preferred pronouns. She also initiated a conversation about why pronoun introductions were important.

Teryn and her parents had been very proactive. They knew with all the news coverage about transgender youth, school bathrooms, and a variety of other issues, they should meet with Principal Trainor before the new school year.

When the issue of bathroom use arose, Principal Trainor asked which bathrooms Teryn wanted to use. "I'm a girl. I want to use the girls' bathrooms," she answered.

"Sounds good. I'll talk school staff through this. Hopefully nobody will give you a hard time."

When the school year began Teryn used the girls' bathrooms. Similar to her general experience as a transgender woman at the school, she withstood some bias, from jokes about her gender identity to suspicious glares. This made her reluctant to use the bathrooms at all. When she reported the instances to Principal Trainor, he said, "Don't worry. People are trying to make sense of things. They need time to get comfortable with the change."

Meanwhile, several parents called to complain to Principal Trainor that they didn't like the idea of a "boy" using a "girl's" bathroom. The principal stood firm. Then those parents started reaching out to the superintendent, Ms. Stoudt, with their complaints. A couple weeks into the school year Ms. Stoudt reached out to Mr. Trainor and insisted he instruct Teryn to use the boys' bathrooms until a new policy could be discussed.

When the principal pressed her on her decision Ms. Stoudt cited concerns about sexual violence. "How would you feel if he attacked one of your female students?" she asked.

Based on what he heard about what other schools were doing related to transgender students and student bathrooms, Mr. Trainor suggested a compromise: "Can we change one of the staff bathrooms into a 'gender-neutral' bathroom, allowing Teryn to use that one?"

Ms. Stoudt agreed, only if the bathroom was located discreetly. "We don't want people feeling uncomfortable walking through the school," she explained.

Relieved, Mr. Trainor printed a sign, "Gender-Neutral Bathroom," and taped it to the door of the staff bathroom behind the choral music room. He emailed staff to announce the change.

Horrified at this "solution," Ms. Harris responded to Mr. Trainor, reminding him, not only that this left Teryn even more vulnerable to a wide variety of humiliations, but also that the bathroom was located too far from her classes for her to use it.

"Sorry, but that's the best we can do," he replied.

Questions

1 What other, more equitable, steps could Mr. Trainor, Ms. Harris, and other teachers take to support Teryn? What are some ways they can educate themselves more thoroughly about transphobia?

2 What role can asking students to name their preferred gender pronouns play in initiating conversations about sexism, transphobia, and other forms of injustice? Are there dangers to this sort of activity in how it might pressure students to identify something publicly they are not comfortable identifying publicly?

3 Both Mr. Trainor and Ms. Stoudt express concern about creating discomfort for people who might harbor transphobia, whether implicit or explicit. Can you recall instances when a school you attended or a school at which you worked prioritized the comfort of people who did not support progress on equity over the comfort and safety of people who were experiencing inequity?

CASE 7.3: TIMMY'S GENDER NONCONFORMITY

Timmy, a student in Ms. Grover's class, often was teased by classmates because he displayed what some interpreted to be "girl" qualities. Ms. Grover had been warned of this situation by Mr. Franks and Ms. Puterio, Timmy's previous teachers. In fact, ever since Kindergarten, teachers and administrators had noticed not only that Timmy preferred to play with girls, but that he preferred what they considered stereotypically "girl" toys and books.

Mr. Franks noted that, as a Kindergartner, Timmy gravitated toward playing with costumes. He especially liked a princess gown and tiara. Other children didn't seem to care, though some made an occasional remark about *those being girls' clothes*. Mr. Franks always stepped in quickly to say that all the clothes and toys were for everybody. Timmy's mother, who picked him up from school and often saw him playing with dresses or carrying around a doll, never mentioned any concerns.

Timmy's first and second grade teachers handled the situation similarly, but noticed the teasing slowly intensifying. Ms. Puterio was quick to defend Timmy. She also noticed that the girls who had been friends with Timmy began to nudge him out of their social circles and join in on the teasing. She spoke with the girls about this, urging them to be nicer, but it didn't help. Timmy, however, did not seem upset about losing friends.

One day, Ms. Grover noticed several students were standing around Timmy's desk, pointing and laughing. "What's going on?" she inquired.

"Timmy's a girl!" one student shouted, eliciting laughter from classmates.

"He painted his fingernails, like a girl," another student giggled.

"It's just *one* nail," Timmy muttered, bending forward and hiding his face in his arms, which were crossed on the desk.

Ms. Grover could see the pinky nail on his left hand was painted white. "Everybody take your seats. There will be no teasing in this classroom."

As the students sat down Ms. Grover kneeled next to Timmy's desk and asked in a whisper, "Do your parents know you painted your fingernail?"

"My mom knows," he whispered back, tears in his eyes. "She only let me paint one."

Ms. Grover felt conflicted. On the one hand, she knew children could be brutal over gender identity and most bullying at school happened beyond the earshot of teachers. She also knew that the staff could not completely protect Timmy from the increasingly harsh bullying he might endure in future years.

Part of her wanted to urge Timmy's parents to help him try to fit in better at school, maybe even help him try to make friends with boys. Another part of her wanted to create a safe environment for Timmy exactly as Timmy was, but she knew that would take a schoolwide effort and she was sure not everybody would be onboard. She also figured she needed to find an educational way to address what was going on with her students despite not fully understanding it herself, and without further alienating Timmy.

Questions

1 Timmy's teachers from Kindergarten through second grade, despite noticing he was being teased more, only chose to intervene by addressing the teasing. Should they have done more, such as educating students about gender identity? In your opinion, is this topic not appropriate in early elementary?

2 How should Ms. Grover broach this conversation with Timmy's parents? Timmy specified that his *mom* knew he had painted his fingernail. Should Ms. Grover reach out to Timmy's mother, specifically, unsure about whether his father knew about the situation?

3 Ms. Grover was unsure about her ability to make the school a welcoming place for Timmy, which led her to wonder whether it might be safer for Timmy to conform while he's at school. What would you advise Ms. Grover to do?

CASE 7.4: ONLINE OBJECTIFICATION

Petra usually was full of energy and smiles, so Ms. Alexandra was surprised Monday morning when Petra walked into her classroom looking somber.

"Are you feeling OK?" Ms. Alexandra asked as Petra headed toward her desk.

"Yeah," Petra answered, avoiding eye contact.

A few minutes later Ms. Alexandra noticed some students smirking at Petra. One of them, Tyler, was holding his phone up so other students could see it. Sensing a connection between Petra's discomfort and whatever Tyler and others were seeing on the screen, Ms. Alexandra approached the group. Tyler quickly slipped the phone into his pocket.

"What's going on, Tyler?" Ms. Alexandra asked.

"Nothing," he replied. "Just checking Facebook."

Ms. Alexandra reminded Tyler that he was only allowed to use his phone to look up information relevant to schoolwork. "If you're on Facebook again I'll take the phone until the end of the day."

She looked back at Petra, whose head was buried in her arms. Concerned, Ms. Alexandra approached Petra and motioned her toward the hallway.

"What is going on?" Ms. Alexandra asked once they were both in the hallway. "I can see you're upset and I want to help, but I can't help if I don't know what's wrong." Petra shook her head. "Is it something on Facebook?" Ms. Alexandra inquired? Petra started crying.

At that moment Ms. Santos, the assistant principal, turned the corner. She was walking quickly toward Ms. Alexandra and Petra, carrying her computer.

"Are you OK?" Ms. Santos asked Petra, handing Ms. Alexandra the computer. A Facebook page titled "Rate the Girls" was on the screen. At the top of the page was a photo of Petra. Beneath the photo was a series of numbers between one and ten and brief comments about Petra's attractiveness such as "was hotter last year" and "ok, nothing special." Ms. Alexandra recognized the names of some, but not all, of the students who left comments.

"Oh no," Ms. Alexandra said, giving Petra a hug.

"I guess that means you don't know that the creator of this page is in your class?" Ms. Santos asked.

"Tyler?" Ms. Alexandra inquired.

Ms. Santos responded, "He posted it on Friday. It's been a different girl every day since then. Some students just reported it."

"Well, I'm going to put an end to this right now," Ms. Alexandra exclaimed as she stepped toward her classroom door.

"Wait!" Petra pleaded. "Please don't say anything. That'll make it worse. Please!"

"OK," Ms. Santos said. "Well, for now why don't you take your seat and let Ms. Alexandra and I chat." Ms. Alexandra and Ms. Santos could hear laughter as Petra walked into the room, making them both cringe and reminding them they had just sent her into a hostile environment.

Ms. Alexandra asked whether this situation was covered under the school's anti-bullying policy.

"Absolutely," Ms. Santos replied, "or at least it should be. My concern is how we can hold Tyler accountable and address this issue with all students without making Petra and the other girls on that Facebook page bigger targets."

Questions

1 How would you respond to Petra's request to not address the incident directly with students because she fears it would escalate the bullying and harassment she is experiencing?

2 Should Ms. Santos remove Tyler from class immediately? What about other students who posted comments?

3 What are some ways you have seen social media used to facilitate bullying, sexual harassment, or other types of bias and discrimination? What role should schools play in addressing these social media concerns?

CASE 7.5: DRESS CODE DISTRESS

Ms. Patil was wandering through the shopping mall with her daughter in a stroller when she saw Angela, one of her students. Angela looked sad and her mom was trying to comfort her. Angela's mom spotted Ms. Patil and nodded. Ms. Patil walked over and asked if everything was all right.

"No, it's not," Angela's mom replied. "We've been shopping for hours and we're having a hard time finding clothes that fit her and don't violate the school's dress code. We're both frustrated!"

Ms. Patil inquired further about the problem. From what she knew of the dress code, finding appropriate clothes shouldn't be difficult. Angela was taller and heavier than most girls her age. Ms. Patil wondered if that could be the part of the problem.

"We spent an hour yesterday talking to the principal about Angela's clothes. My daughter had to sit in the office and listen to people talk about her body. It humiliated her. A teacher sent her to the office. She told Angela boys were distracted by her clothes because they were too tight."

Ms. Patil was puzzled. "What were you wearing?" she asked Angela.

"Leggings and a t-shirt," she answered.

Her mother jumped in, "I wonder whether you all know how hard it is to shop for girls who don't have small body types. I can't afford many of the clothes we do find. She's teased by classmates for wearing clothes that are too baggy. We experienced similar challenges shopping for a Homecoming dress for Angela's older sister. There are so many restrictions!"

Ms. Patil was taken aback by this outpouring of frustration, but appreciated the candor. She never personally struggled with finding clothes that adhered to the dress code, but she occasionally read news stories or blog posts by parents and students sharing similar frustrations. "How can I help?" she asked.

"It would be great if you could talk to the other teachers," Angela asked softly. "Do something about the dress code. Sometimes I don't want to go to school at all."

"I'm so sorry you're experiencing this. I'm especially sorry for that uncomfortable situation in the office," answered Ms. Patil. "I will definitely look into the dress code. And I'll keep this conversation private."

"This isn't just an issue for Angela. Imagine how many other girls have been humiliated by these kinds of dress codes. Nobody is talking about how all these restrictions are getting in the way of *girls'* learning," Angela's mom added.

"I'll do my best," Ms. Patil reassured her before giving Angela a comforting hug. As they walked away, Ms. Patil looked at her daughter in the stroller. She sighed and thought to herself, *I need to help make a change not only for current students but also for you.*

Questions

1 Angela's mom explained that it's difficult for Angela to adhere to the dress code because of her body type. Why else might it be difficult for students to adhere to dress codes?

2 The purpose of dress codes often is to prevent distractions from learning. How might dress code policies contribute to body-shaming instead? How might other students contribute to body-shaming? How can both factors be addressed?

3 Dress code enforcement can be subjective. How might this subjectivity create inequitable experiences within schools?

8

CASES ON (DIS)ABILITY

CASE 8.1: A "SURPRISE" FIRE DRILL

Ms. Stintson, a special education teacher, enjoyed helping colleagues understand the unique needs of students with whom she worked. Recently, though, she sensed frustration on the part of Ms. Foster, who recently received a new student with an Individualized Education Plan (IEP) in her class.

Aiden had been diagnosed with an Autism Spectrum Disorder but functioned well in a mainstream classroom. Ms. Foster believed many of the IEP objectives were unnecessary because Aiden was progressing just as well as his peers. She often expressed this sentiment with other teachers. Ms. Stintson reminded her she needed to follow the plan, but also mentioned that teachers are welcome to share concerns during the annual IEP review.

One morning, the principal pulled Ms. Stintson aside and informed her he would administer a surprise fire drill later that morning. He asked her to take necessary measures to ensure her students would not be negatively affected by the drill.

One of the first students Ms. Stintson thought about was Aiden. His parents had indicated loud noises scared him so much they could disrupt his entire week. Although this concern was not yet indicated in his IEP, Aiden's parents had asked Ms. Stintson if she could notify Aiden about fire drills before they occurred and provide him with noise-reducing headphones.

Ms. Stintson stopped by Ms. Foster's classroom to share the plan with her. "I'll sneak in a minute or so before the alarm to give Aiden the headphones, then walk with him out of the school with the rest of the students," Ms. Stintson explained.

Ms. Foster immediately expressed concern about this arrangement. "It isn't a *surprise* fire drill if the students see you preparing Aiden for it," she complained. "The best thing we can do for *all* of them is to make the drill as authentic as possible." She continued: "Plus, it's not mandated in Aiden's IEP. You wouldn't be able to come in and give him headphones if there was a *real* fire."

Ms. Stintson reminded Ms. Foster of Aiden's parents' request. She mentioned the potentially severe consequences for Aiden if he is taken by surprise and subjected to the noise and chaos of a fire drill. "I understand your desire to make it authentic," she explained, "but we can't knowingly subject Aiden to a harmful experience."

"I'll be discreet," Ms. Stintson continued. "It is in Aiden's best interest to remain with his classmates so he will be prepared if there is a real fire."

"Sorry," Ms. Foster responded curtly. "If you think headphones are necessary, then you'll need to take him out of my classroom before the drill so other students don't suspect anything. That's my best compromise. I need to keep all my students' safety in mind."

Ms. Foster left the room before Ms. Stintson could respond.

Ms. Stintson's impulse was to notify the principal about Ms. Foster's unwillingness to help, but she worried about how that might affect future interactions with Ms. Foster. And of course, she certainly did not want Ms. Foster to resent having Aiden in class.

Questions

1 Do you agree with Ms. Stintson, who is concerned primarily about how a fire drill might impact Aiden, or with Ms. Foster, who worries that the accommodation will make the experience less authentic to him and other students? Why? To what extent do the wishes of Aiden's parents inform your opinion?

2 What might you have recommended to Ms. Stintson and Ms. Foster as an alternative compromise, or is a compromise not an option in this case?

3 Sometimes, especially when co-teaching is involved, educators "choose their battles" with their co-workers. Is this a case where Ms. Stintson should prioritize her professional relationship over advocating for Aiden? Have you ever needed to make a similar decision?

CASE 8.2: INSUFFICIENT ACCOMMODATIONS

One of Ms. Thurston's favorite activities was taking students to Meadow Creek Park, a nearby nature reserve, where they could explore the same trails and terrain as ecologists from the local university. She was especially excited this year because the park had hired a new education director, Ms. Parsons, who had designed a one-mile conservation hike specifically for students. Ms. Thurston couldn't wait to take students on that hike.

Two weeks before the fieldtrip, a new student, Justin, was added to Ms. Thurston's class. Justin had cerebral palsy, a condition that required him to use crutches. At first Ms. Thurston was concerned about whether Justin would be able to participate in the fieldtrip. Although he navigated the classroom and school easily, Ms. Thurston was not sure whether the learning center in the park was accessible. Certainly, it met basic Americans with Disabilities Act standards with ramps, accessible parking, and wheelchair accessible bathrooms, but these were minimal standards.

Ms. Thurston called Ms. Parsons to inquire about the accommodations offered for students like Justin. Ms. Parsons assured Ms. Thurston, saying, "The hike might be a bit much for Justin, but we have accommodations for students with physical disabilities and learning differences. He'll be fine."

When the bus pulled up to the Meadow Creek learning center, Ms. Parsons was there to greet them. As the students listened to their short lesson and asked the tour guides questions, Ms. Thurston talked with Ms. Parsons about accommodations for Justin. "Looks like he can spend some time in the garden," Ms. Thurston said.

"Unfortunately, park rules don't allow for that," Ms. Parsons responded. She pointed to a sign labeled "General Rules of the Reserve."

The third rule read: "For their own safety, visitors with conditions, injuries, or illnesses that may impair their mobility are not permitted on the nature paths or in the gardens. A selection of films about local ecology are available for people who are unable to participate in the hikes due to these conditions."

Shocked, Ms. Thurston replied, "I thought you said you had accommodations. A film isn't an accommodation!"

Heading back toward the students, Ms. Thurston wondered what to do next. Should she use this as a teachable moment? What should she say to Justin? How could she still make it a meaningful experience for him?

Questions

1 Ms. Thurston was frustrated to find that the learning "accommodation" for Justin consisted of sitting *inside* the center and watching a film while his classmates hiked. In your estimation, does this constitute an equitable accommodation? If not, what sorts of accommodations might have been more equitable?

2 Is it Ms. Thurston's responsibility to provide the hike experience to most of her students even if one was to be excluded from any sort of parallel learning opportunity? Should she look for a different learning opportunity that could include all her students, even if she feels that opportunity might not generate the same enthusiasm for most of her students as hiking in Meadow Creek Park?

3 How, as she approaches her students after talking with Ms. Parsons, might Ms. Thurston use this situation as a teachable moment for *all* her students? Can she do so without risking making Justin uncomfortable?

CASE 8.3: NUT ALLERGY

Talia had a nut allergy that required extra precautions to ensure her safety while at school. Her teachers, including Mr. Hughes, willingly made accommodations so Talia never felt like she was missing out due to her medical concerns. Some of these accommodations included having all students wash their hands diligently before returning from lunch and making sure students did not bring snacks from home into the classroom. He clearly communicated his "nut-free" policy to all his students' families, and also sought training from the school nurse on how to use an epinephrine auto-injector, which he could use to administer medication if necessary.

At the beginning of the school year, Talia's mom, Ms. Thomas, asked Mr. Hughes if she could chaperone all the class's field trips so she would be present if Talia experienced an allergic reaction. Mr. Hughes agreed, but also mentioned that parents typically attended only one field trip during the year so other parents also would have an opportunity to chaperone. He warned her some might complain about her request, but said he would support her.

"Talia's safety is more important than people's misperceptions," Ms. Thomas replied. Mr. Hughes appreciated her advocacy for Talia.

When Mr. Hughes sent home permission slips for field trips and requests for chaperones he was mindful to reduce the number of chaperones he needed by one to reserve a spot for Ms. Thomas. He received occasional complaints about why she was permitted to attend multiple trips, but he was quick to point out how helpful it was to have Ms. Thomas on the trips so he could focus on the rest of the students.

Then he sent home permission slips and chaperone requests for the last field trip of the year: a visit to the state capitol building. The day he sent permission slips home, Mr. Hughes learned his class had been invited to watch their governor deliver a live press conference. They would even have time to ask her questions and take photos with her.

Due to security restrictions at the governor's office, only a few parents could chaperone. Mr. Hughes received several emails from interested parents who insisted they should chaperone because they hadn't attended previous trips. Regretfully, Mr. Hughes had to deny most requests.

The next day, as he took morning attendance, he noticed Talia looked unusually sad. "What's wrong, Talia?" he asked.

Talia responded that classmates were being mean to her because their parents could not chaperone. "They're mad because my mom *has to come*."

"It's just an excuse," one of Talia's classmates said. "We've never seen you get sick from nuts."

Mr. Hughes was shocked, and decided to address this issue with the whole class. This prompted candid responses from students, many of whom said their parents had been complaining at home.

Mr. Hughes glanced at Talia, who looked embarrassed. *I'm not going to change my policy*, he thought, *but I definitely need to do something differently*.

Questions

1 Were Mr. Hughes' accommodations for Talia, such as allowing her mother to chaperone every field trip, necessary or just considerate?

2 Mr. Hughes was committed to maintaining an equitable environment in his classroom. Given his students' comments about Talia and the fact that they might have been hearing negative things about Talia and her mother at home, how should he have addressed this situation in the classroom?

3 What policies exist in your class, school, or district, or in other districts, pertaining to nut allergies or similar medical conditions? What else could schools do to ensure the safety of students who are diagnosed with a food allergy?

CASE 8.4: BEHAVIOR MANAGEMENT MISSING THE MARK

"This new system is just not working," Mr. Paulson heard his colleague, Mr. Rhett, exclaim in frustration. They were eating lunch in the staff lounge.

"Some of these students *need* to be suspended," he continued. "Instead we are keeping them in school, allowing them to disrupt other students' learning. It's a disservice to everyone, including the teachers."

This wasn't the first time Mr. Paulson had heard this sentiment from one of his peers. Over the summer, upon analyzing data about which students were more likely to be sent to the office, administration implemented a new reward system to help with behavior issues. Mr. Paulson watched as resentment and frustration grew among the staff. They were more hesitant to send students out of the class for fear of over-reporting, but were unsure how to handle some significant behavior issues in class.

That afternoon after school Mr. Paulson stopped by Mr. Rhett's classroom to offer some help. Mr. Paulson typically had a good rapport with students. During their conversation, Mr. Paulson learned that two students, Andre and Carson, had been cursing at their teacher and other classmates.

"Other students tease each other but those two take it to the next level," Mr. Rhett complained. He said he was aware both boys received special education services. This made him even more hesitant to send them to the office, as the administration was monitoring office referrals. Instead, Mr. Rhett offered Andre and Carson incentives based on the new reward system. He hoped this positive intervention would curb the unwanted behavior. Unfortunately, from Mr. Rhett's perspective, neither student seemed interested in earning rewards. They continued to be disruptive.

Mr. Paulson knew both students had a history of behavior concerns and, as a result, a reputation among the staff, but he was typically successful finding ways to resolve minor concerns within the class and rarely needed to send them to the office. He told Mr. Rhett he would speak with the students personally.

The next day, Mr. Paulson was surprised at how candid Andre and Carson were with him about their behavior. They explained that Mr. Paulson engaged them as learners, allowed them to express themselves and even to move around. His class was a break from the frustrations they felt at school.

"The other students make fun of us because we're in Special Ed," Andre explained.

"And most teachers ignore it," Carson added. "So we handle it ourselves."

"Why do we have to behave in a school we hate?" Andre asked angrily.

"In a school that hates *us*," Carson added.

Mr. Paulson wasn't sure how to respond to Andre and Carson. He also wasn't sure what he should share with Mr. Rhett and the rest of his colleagues.

Questions

1 Why might Andre and Caron appear unmotivated by the schoolwide reward system? What other strategies could Mr. Rhett have tried?

2 The intent of the administration's desire to change the behavior system and office referrals was positive, but the impact on staff and students was negative. Why might this be the case? What changes could be made to address the negative outcomes?

3 How would you respond to Andre's question if you were Mr. Rhett? Do you think there are students in your school or district who feel the same way? If so, what should be done to address those concerns?

9

CASES ON SEXUAL ORIENTATION

CASE 9.1: A NEW CLUB

Ms. Green was a proponent of student efficacy. Many students at Halloway School who felt alienated or disconnected gravitated toward Ms. Green and her classroom.

It was little surprise, then, when Lorraine and Jeff, the only two "out" lesbian, gay, bisexual, or queer (LGBQ) students at the school, asked Ms. Green if she would serve as faculty sponsor for a Gay-Straight Alliance or "GSA," a student organization for LGBQ students and their allies. They wanted to create a student group that could be a "safe space" for LGBQ students, and shared that Terrence and Hu, two classmates who identified as heterosexual but were allies, wanted to help start the GSA also. "We've already started talking about how to help educate our peers about homophobia," Lorraine explained. "We've even researched GSAs at other schools."

"Sounds like you've done your homework," Ms. Green replied.

"It's a nationwide movement," Lorraine added.

"Then I'll be your sponsor," Ms. Green said. Nothing excited her more than students initiating these sorts of efforts. Usually students who came to her with requests did so in search of permission or with the assumption that Ms. Green would lead the charge. Lorraine and Jeff were taking the lead, not seeking permission.

Of course, Ms. Green knew that Lorraine, Jeff, Terrence, and Hu were heading down a difficult road; that their efforts might be met with ridicule from some peers and calls to the school from angry parents. But she agreed to support them any way she could.

A few days later Ms. Livingsworth, Halloway's principal, visited Ms. Green's classroom. At first she sounded supportive of the students' efforts. "I think it's great when young people take initiative," she said. "They're braver than I was at their age."

"I do have a concern about this particular group, though," Ms. Livingsworth continued. "We talk about being inclusive. My fear is, by allowing a Gay-Straight Alliance, we might be alienating conservative families whose religious views don't approve of homosexuality."

"Those families feel welcome here in other ways," Ms. Green insisted. "The students are just trying to create space for themselves as people who care about ending discrimination."

Ms. Livingsworth nodded. "I commend them for that. But it's not the right time for a GSA. Let's suggest they start a Diversity Club instead. That way all students will feel included."

Ms. Green knew this would devastate Lorraine and Jeff. She felt horribly disappointed, too, but knew Principal Livingsworth had made a final decision. Eventually she would need to raise this issue again, but for now she needed to focus on breaking the news to the students.

Questions

1 Was Ms. Livingsworth's suggestion that Lorraine and her peers start a Diversity Club rather than a GSA an equitable one? Why or why not? How is a Diversity Club different in nature from a GSA?

2 If you were in Ms. Green's shoes, would you have argued more vigorously in support of the GSA? If so, how?

3 What ways can Ms. Green support the students' efforts to create a safer community for themselves, while also complying with Ms. Livingsworth's request?

CASE 9.2: DATE AUCTION

During a student council meeting at Dorothy Day High School, Jonathan, council president, introduced the idea of hosting a fundraiser for a local homeless shelter. Historically, Dorothy Day's students had been predominantly white and upper-middle class. However, as Jonathan reminded his classmates, the school's population was growing increasingly diverse racially and economically. "I hate when people think we're a bunch of rich white kids," he said. "Here's something we can do to change that perception." The council voted in favor of hosting the fundraiser.

Council members brainstormed fundraising ideas. Their advisor, Mr. Petrov, believed in students taking ownership of their own projects, so he asserted his voice minimally during meetings.

One student, Tanya, suggested a "Date Auction" in which students could bid on an opportunity to go on a date with select members of the senior class. She had read about another school hosting a similar event. "It generated a *lot* of money and cost next to nothing," she explained. She added that the dates could be arranged to occur simultaneously in a local restaurant, ensuring student safety and mitigating discomfort participants might experience.

The students discussed the event enthusiastically. "Everyone will love this!" Jonathan said to a chorus of nods.

When time came to identify volunteers to be auctioned and generate bidding interest, Tanya recommended Nate, another council member. "Everyone knows Nate and everybody *loves* Nate," she said. Nate agreed, joking he would win the highest bids.

Jonathan joked that Nate would probably get bids "from girls *and from guys*" who would want a date with him, eliciting laughs from several council members.

Nate responded, "Whatever! I'm not gay. Even if it's for charity, I'm quitting if a guy bids on me." While some council members continued laughing, others changed the topic to restaurants that might be willing to donate meals.

As the meeting was coming to a close, Tanya asked Mr. Petrov if it would be all right for the student council to stipulate that bids would only be considered if made by "students of the opposite sex from the students being auctioned off." She hoped this stipulation would help "avoid that kind of situation."

The council members looked at Mr. Petrov, waiting for a response.

Questions

1 Keeping in mind that Mr. Petrov believed students should take ownership of their projects, at which point and how should he have intervened?

2 Using students' conversation, identify different types of bias and inequity that are present in this case.

3 The council thought everyone would love this idea. Among the student population, who might feel offended or alienated by a Date Auction?

CASE 9.3: OUTED AT SCHOOL

Mr. Brooks never intended to move back to his hometown, a place where gay men like him were reminded constantly they were not welcome. However, his mother had been diagnosed with cancer, so he moved home to care for her. Luckily, a neighborhood school had an opening for a teacher.

When he was offered the position by Principal Patterson, he decided reluctantly to mention his sexual orientation. "I'm telling you this because I know this area can be rough for people like me. I can handle it, but I can't handle not having support from leadership."

Ms. Patterson responded, "It's not every day somebody divulges his sexual identity in an interview. Since you brought it up, do you mind me asking how you'll handle it with students?"

"If you're asking whether I'll be 'out' at work, the answer is *no way*. Not here."

"If you need my support, you have it," Ms. Patterson said.

This brought Mr. Brooks some relief. Still, when he remembered his experience as a closeted gay student, he shuddered. Memories weighed on him of classmates' *constant* use of phrases like "that's so gay," and the bullying doled out to students who did not conform to binary gender identities. Worse were memories of unresponsive adults in his schools. *Maybe things have changed*, he thought.

The first couple months of the school year went smoothly. Mr. Brooks heard the occasional offensive comment and the usual heteronormative assumptions, like questions about whether he had a girlfriend. Overall, however, it was friendlier than he anticipated, though he hated having to hide who he was.

Then, in late fall, Mr. Brooks was stunned when Jeremy, one of his more boisterous students, asked him in front of the class if he was gay.

This was not a new question for him, so the asking did not faze him so much as the collective gasp of the students. He knew what he *should* say: *That is not an appropriate thing to ask your teacher.* Instead, he calmly asked, "Why would you ask that?"

"My brother told me. He saw it on Facebook," Jeremy said.

"How many of you have heard about this?" Mr. Brooks asked. Most of his students raised their hands. "I will not discuss my personal life," he said. "Let's focus on today's material."

Mr. Brooks was disappointed with how he'd handled Jeremy's question. Part of him wished he'd said, "I'm gay and it is sad to think how much better I could teach if I didn't have to spend energy hiding it." Then he remembered where he was and how he needed that job.

When school ended he went to see Ms. Patterson. "Guess what happened today," he said.

"I can only guess," she responded. "It's all over social media. Some parents already requested I move their children out of your class."

"What did you say?" Mr. Brooks asked.

"I said your sexual orientation is irrelevant to your teaching," she replied. "I refused to move their children."

"I appreciate that. What now?" Mr. Brooks asked. "I can't lie about this to my students. Hiding it is one thing, but lying is something else."

"I wouldn't ask you to lie," Ms. Patterson said, "so let's figure this out together."

Questions

1   Should Jeremy be punished for asking Mr. Brooks about his sexual orientation?

2   Although things were better at first than Mr. Brooks anticipated, he still was subject to "heteronormative assumptions." In a heteronormative context, people are assumed to be heterosexual and heterosexuality is deemed "normal," even if implicitly so. What are some of the ways in which you have witnessed heteronormativity in schools?

3   How should Mr. Brooks address the rumors with his students? To what extent should attitudes in the school or wider community dictate how he handles the situation?

CASE 9.4: TWO MOMS

Ms. Ribiero was no fan of controversy, but she was attuned to students' needs. So when she learned that Denise, who lived with her two mothers, would be in her class, she did some research. She found two highly recommended books depicting families with same-sex parents for her classroom library. She had no intention of teaching a lesson on same-sex partners. She just felt the books should be available to Denise. Denise's moms appreciated her thoughtfulness.

A couple months into the school year Ms. Ribiero noticed a few students briefly looking at one of those books, then one day she noticed Denise reading one of the books. One of Denise's classmates, Julia, asked her what she was reading.

"It's called *Emma and Meesha My Boy: A Two-Mom Story*," Denise replied.

"What's it about?"

Without skipping a beat Denise said, "A little girl who lives with her two moms and they have a cat." Overhearing their conversation, Ms. Ribiero walked toward them.

"Two moms?" Julia asked, voice elevated, grabbing the attention of nearby classmates. "Her moms live together? Weird."

Brandon pointed to Denise and said, "*She's* reading a book about weird people."

"OK Julia and Brandon," Ms. Ribiero interrupted, "focus on your books and let Denise focus on hers."

Immediately Ms. Ribiero regretted her response, but she was uneasy about doing anything that might seem controversial. She did not feel comfortable or prepared to teach a mini-lesson on family diversity or same-sex partners on the spot.

She agonized that evening over what to do. She needed to do *something*, not necessarily as a matter of marriage rights or explicit advocacy for lesbian or gay people, but as a matter of accuracy. Families with two moms *do exist*. Plus, although Denise was the only student in class with same-sex parents, others lived in a variety of family structures.

Ms. Ribiero decided to read *Emma and Meesha My Boy* aloud to the class the next day. Because she was using the book to begin a conversation about family diversity rather than "gay marriage," she decided to not send home notices so families could opt their children out of the activity.

She was thrilled to see how open students were about the book. "Your family is like that?" Julia asked Denise.

"Yes. Two moms," Denise replied.

As other students began asking Denise questions, Ms. Ribiero felt tempted to stop the conversation. But she paused, happy with how respectful the students were being with one another and how empowered Denise appeared as she answered questions.

She was happy, that is, until the next morning, when she learned from Principal Hernandez that several parents called complaining that she was teaching about "homosexuality" and "gay marriage."

Mr. Hernandez shared, "A few are angry. They're coming by after school."

Ms. Ribiero anxiously said, "All I did was read a book about a girl with two moms."

"I know you're the last person who would purposefully start a firestorm. Come to the office after school. The parents are arriving around 3:45."

"Thank you," Ms. Ribiero said nervously before heading to her classroom.

Questions

1 How else could Ms. Ribiero have responded when she saw Julia and Brandon giving Denise a hard time about reading a book about a child with two moms?

2 What responsibility do we, as educators, have to educate students about diverse family structures, including families with same-sex parents? What responsibility do we have to educate students about discrimination and inequity on the basis of sexual orientation?

3 Did Mr. Hernandez do the right thing by inviting Ms. Ribiero into the conversation with parents? How should he and Ms. Ribiero respond to the parents' complaints?

10

CASES ON LANGUAGE

CASE 10.1: STUDENT INTERPRETER

"Wait, Maria!" Mr. Clark shouted. He hurried to catch up with Maria, her mother, and her younger sister, Marcella, as they left school at the end of the day. Maria usually walked home with her sister. They were delighted that day when their mother arrived to walk them home.

Mr. Clark had been trying to reach Maria's mother, Ms. Montes, to discuss discipline concerns about Maria. Several classmates had reported that Maria called them names. Maria denied the accusations, but Mr. Clark started paying closer attention to Maria's interactions with classmates and witnessed a couple incidents.

He wrote a note home but noticed a few days later it remained in Maria's backpack, undelivered. Then he called her parents, but he knew they were just learning English so he wasn't confident they understood his message. As he jogged to catch up with Ms. Montes, Mr. Clark wondered how their conversation would go. He didn't speak Spanish and didn't have an interpreter.

When he caught up with the group, Mr. Clark shook Ms. Montes's hand and asked if she had a few minutes to talk. "Yes," she replied, hesitantly. Mr. Clark noticed that Maria's happy expression quickly changed. He knew it would not be a good idea to ask Maria to interpret. He was not sure she would translate accurately given the topic. He turned instead to Marcella, asking if she would translate. Marcella nodded and explained to her mother that Mr. Clark needed to talk about Maria's behavior.

After several minutes of conversation, Maria, Ms. Montes, and Mr. Clark generally covered the behavior concerns and agreed to meet again with an interpreter if needed. Mr. Clark was pleased with the results of the impromptu meeting. "Thank you, Marcella," he said, and told her how wonderful her English was. He looked at Maria's mom and said, "You must be very proud of her."

Marcella beamed. "I can help other teachers too," she said. Mr. Clark smiled and said he might need her help translating for her mother again soon.

Maria and Ms. Montes appeared uncomfortable. Mr. Clark reassured them, "I know next time we will have something good to report."

"I'll see you tomorrow, Maria," he said with a wave, then headed back toward the school.

Mr. Clark felt satisfied about what he accomplished in the meeting. He felt confident Ms. Montes would follow through on their agreement to meet if needed. As a bonus, he felt good about empowering Marcella and praising her for her help. He was happy to know she would be a resource to translate for her mother if he could not arrange for an interpreter.

A win-win, he thought.

Questions

1 Why might Ms. Montes and Maria have been uncomfortable with Mr. Clark's interaction with Marcella?

2 In your opinion, was it appropriate for Mr. Clark to stop Ms. Montes, Maria, and Marcella on their walk home from school in order to have a conversation about Maria's behavior? Why or why not?

3 What other strategies might Mr. Clark have used to reach Maria's parents?

CASE 10.2: ENGLISH-ONLY

When Ms. Mancini attended Potomac School, the students and teachers were almost all white. She could not remember one classmate who spoke a language other than English at home. By the time Ms. Mancini applied for a teaching job at Potomac, more than one-third of the students spoke languages other than English at home.

Although she only spoke English, Ms. Mancini often teamed with Ms. de Leon, a teacher with a Teaching English to Speakers of Other Languages endorsement. In addition to speaking English, Ms. de Leon spoke fluent Spanish and learned phrases from the other languages students spoke.

Unfortunately, it was not uncommon for some other teachers to lament changes in the student population or complain that students' families were not learning English. Aside from Ms. de Leon, she found few teachers willing to openly advocate for English Language Learners.

During a faculty meeting, a small group of teachers collectively introduced their concerns about "the ELLs." Ms. Ross was particularly outspoken. "It's one thing for them to speak their languages at lunch, but not in my classroom. It's a distraction!"

"Exactly!" Mr. Thompson agreed. "They could be talking about other students or something else inappropriate."

"I'm sure that's not the case," Ms. Mancini interjected, but she was drowned out by what seemed like years of pent-up frustration from other teachers.

"It's their parents," Ms. Ross said. "They don't learn English and that hinders their children's ability to learn it."

"I used to be one of those students," Ms. de Leon responded. "When you talk about *those kids* you're talking about me. And I can tell you, you are way off base."

Sensing tension, Mr. Stintson, the principal, stepped in. "I don't like how contentious this is getting. We're all colleagues." He then explained how he had been feeling pressure from district administration to institute the same English-only policies adopted by other schools. "This wouldn't affect what students do in their free time or while receiving language services," he explained, "but it will mean, during classroom time, students will *not* be allowed to speak any language except English."

As many of Ms. Mancini's colleagues expressed relief, all she could do was think of her students. She knew their home languages were invaluable to them during class, since they helped one another understand concepts that were unclear in English. She glanced at Ms. de Leon, who looked upset. "Are you saying this is what we're going to do?" Ms. Mancini asked.

"Starting next term, so that we have time to decide how to address student noncompliance," Mr. Stintson answered.

Ms. Mancini knew this was bad policy. She knew it was going to hurt English Language Learners and that it was already alienating Ms. de Leon. She wondered if she could follow a policy she knew would negatively impact student engagement?

Questions

1 Should Ms. Mancini enforce the policy and support the administration's decision, even though she believes it is bad for her students, or should she attempt to change her colleagues' minds? If you believe she should do the latter, how should she go about it?

2 Would you have reached out to Ms. de Leon following the faculty meeting? If so, how?

3 If you were in a school in which an English-only policy was instituted, how might you engage students in a conversation about the policy and its implications, recognizing that students from families who do not speak English at home could feel alienated by the policy?

CASE 10.3: FAMILY NIGHT

In order to bolster family engagement among English Language Learning (ELL) families, Crestview School decided to host a Family Night. Teachers and administrators discussed ways to entice as many people as possible to attend. A light dinner and student performances would draw a crowd, they hoped. The school sent home fliers translated into the languages spoken in the homes of each student. They arranged for students to perform the songs they learned in music classes. Teachers planned a presentation about how to reinforce math concepts at home by utilizing online resources, which was to follow the student performances.

The entire event would last only one hour, they decided, sensitive to the fact that many of their students' parents worked evening shifts or had other responsibilities that made long school events difficult to attend. Mr. Nelson, a veteran teacher, took it upon himself to create a handout about how to access online math tools.

The evening of Family Night, several families began arriving shortly before the published start time. The teachers noticed, however, that most early arrivers were families that regularly attended school events. Five minutes after the scheduled start time, with several people seated and awaiting the performance but several other families not yet in attendance, the teachers decided to change the order of the program, moving their discussion of home support for math learning to the beginning, to be followed by the student performance.

The teachers were relieved to see more families filing into the event as they were speaking. *This is a great turnout*, thought Mr. Nelson. He and several other teachers noticed that several families of ELL students stood in the back of the cafeteria rather than joining other families in the provided seats. Many were chatting. Several parents who arrived early and were sitting seemed visibly annoyed with the background noise.

Ten minutes after the event ended, many of the ELL families continued chatting. Ms. Stowe, a newer teacher, noticed several copies of the handout Mr. Nelson created left on the table so she handed one to each adult who did not have one. She felt disappointed that so few of the parents took time to ask questions when she handed it to them.

Once everybody left, several teachers met briefly to discuss the evening. Ms. Stowe expressed discontent over what she interpreted as disinterest on the parts of many ELL families. Other teachers complained that the evening was not a success because many of the ELL families arrived late and seemed more interested in side conversations than the presentation.

Mr. Nelson could tell his coworkers were discouraged. He knew it would reinforce stereotypes they had about certain families. He also knew the evening held an important lesson for the school, but he was not sure what that lesson was.

Questions

1 Do you agree with the teachers' conclusion that the evening was not a success? Why or why not?

2 The teachers were careful to try to alleviate some potential barriers to participation for ELL families, such as language used in the fliers. What else, if anything, might they have done to make the evening as engaging as possible?

3 Why might some families have remained in the back of the cafeteria rather than joining other families in provided seats? Should the teachers have intervened when some of the seated families grew frustrated with the noise from their conversations? If so, how?

CASE 10.4: A NEW TASK FORCE

Ms. Ahmed, an educational assistant at Pike School, enjoyed speaking Somali with students and families who were bilingual. One morning, she overheard a conversation between two teachers regarding an important after-school meeting later that day. The teachers, Ms. Bayfield and Mr. Dawson, asked Ms. Ahmed whether she was planning to attend.

"I'm sorry," she replied, "I don't know which meeting you're talking about."

Ms. Bayfield explained the purpose of the meeting was to create a task force consisting of district administrators, school staff, and parents to address pressing issues in the school. "Unfortunately," she said. "Our test scores are below the district average. We have a large concentration of students whose home language is not English. The state department of education is threatening to intervene if we don't raise those scores."

"Oh, no," said Ms. Ahmed. "I'll be there, but I wish I had known about the meeting earlier."

Mr. Dawson replied, "It's been posted on the school website and it was listed under 'volunteer opportunities' in the last newsletter. We even sent home translated fliers." The bell rang, so Mr. Dawson and Ms. Bayfield headed to their classrooms. Ms. Ahmed texted her family that she would be at work later than usual.

As she headed to the media center after school, Ms. Ahmed hoped to see some of the other Somali parents, some of whom had expressed concerns to her about the school's performance. Upon entering the meeting, she saw one parent, Mr. Webb, and went to sit by him. As people continued to arrive, Ms. Ahmed realized she and Mr. Webb were the only people present who were not Pike teachers or administrators or people from the district office.

Also present was a consultant, Scott, who started the meeting by explaining that attendees would develop a plan over four meetings. He thanked everyone, saying, "The people in this room will make significant changes to Pike so *all* students can succeed."

Mr. Webb leaned over to Ms. Ahmed and whispered, "Where are the other parents?" Ms. Ahmed shook her head, and then raised her hand to express her concerns. She shared her belief that more parents, especially those who identified with the groups being discussed by the task force, should be part of the decision-making.

A district administrator, Mr. Clark, responded, "While it would be great to have more voices here, the reality with most task forces like this is that some parents are too busy to attend all the meetings or choose not to come because of language barriers."

Scott, wanting to reassure Ms. Ahmed, reminded her that the flier was sent home in multiple languages. "All parents had equal opportunities to learn about the meeting. We need to work with the people who show up. Perhaps you can speak on their behalf."

Ms. Ahmed did not want to speak on behalf of other families and felt her concerns were being dismissed. But she also was worried that if she pushed her concerns any harder she would be perceived as a troublemaker.

Questions

1 Were the strategies used to announce the meeting sufficient to ensure adequate parent representation on the task force? What other strategies, both in terms of announcing the task force and scheduling the first meeting, might have yielded greater attendance?

2 Consider decision-making groups in your school or district. Are they representative of the student population? Are meetings made accessible to the full diversity of families? Is consistent attendance at meetings valued more than adequate family representation?

3 Ms. Ahmed worried that if she pressed the issue of representation she would jeopardize her credibility and be interpreted as a troublemaker. In what other contexts might people worry that insisting on equity might result in being viewed as troublemakers or having their concerns dismissed? Have you experienced such a situation?

11

CASES ON IMMIGRANT STATUS

CASE 11.1: AN ASSIGNED NICKNAME

It was the first day of school at Treetop Elementary. Ms. Goodwin looked forward to meeting her students. She always felt excited on the first day of school, but she found the challenge of learning to pronounce students' names quite stressful. The student body was becoming more ethnically and linguistically diverse each year, and each year she had more and more students whose names she struggled to pronounce correctly.

Once class started, she invited students to sit in a circle on the floor. "Let's learn about one another," she said, asking students to share their names and favorite animals. As students said their names, Ms. Goodwin repeated them, a strategy for learning names quickly. Despite her attentiveness, Ms. Goodwin found herself stumbling over the name of a student named Sarai (pronounced Să-ră-ē).

Over the next couple days Ms. Goodwin noticed she was avoiding saying Sarai's name. She decided to ask Sarai for help. Sarai tried to help, saying her name slowly. As Ms. Goodwin continued to struggle pronouncing it, she worried Sarai was becoming uncomfortable.

Another student, Sara, was standing nearby. She looked at Sarai and said, "Our names are almost the same! Maybe you can be called Sara too so it's easier to say."

"OK." Sarai replied. Ms. Goodwin asked Sarai if she was *sure* this would be OK. Sarai agreed. Ms. Goodwin assured her, "Sara is a pretty name too."

For the next several weeks Sarai was introduced, and introduced herself, to students and staff as "Sara."

When it came time for conferences, Ms. Goodwin, forgetting "Sara" was not Sarai's given name, noticed confusion on her mother's face when she referred to her as "Sara." She explained to Sarai's mother that some students in class have nicknames. "Sarai said it was OK to call her 'Sara,'" Ms. Goodwin explained. "I'm sorry for not checking with you first, but hopefully it's OK."

Sarai's mother seemed hesitant at first, then nodded. Relieved, Ms. Goodwin continued with the conference. She noticed, however, that Sarai's mother seemed quieter and not as engaged as she was earlier.

Questions

1 It is possible that Sarai agreed to change her name even if she did not really want to be called "Sara." Why might this be the case?

2 How might Ms. Goodwin have introduced the topic of Sarai's nickname in a way that invited her mother to share concerns she might have had? When should she have invited Sarai's parents into such a conversation?

3 Why is it so important for teachers to learn to pronounce every student's full given name? Does this depend on the grade of the student or whether the student asks to be called by a name that might be easier for some teachers and classmates to pronounce?

CASE 11.2: I'M NOT BLACK

Ms. Lee enjoyed the growing racial and religious diversity of her students. There were some tensions in the larger community, and sometimes those tensions found their way into the school. For the most part, though, it appeared to her as though students got along well.

Ms. Lee often attempted to create opportunities for students to collaborate in pairs or small groups to help facilitate relationship-building across racial and ethnic groups. She watched happily as students discussed historical narratives or complex political issues together, learning from one another's perspectives.

Recently, however, Ms. Lee and her colleagues began noticing what appeared to be steadily growing conflict at the school between the Nigerian students, most of whom were recent immigrants, and the African American students. A couple brief shoving incidents between these two groups had occurred recently and social divisions were becoming more pronounced.

Late in the school year a new student, Abiola, was assigned to Ms. Lee's class. As she always did for students who joined her classes mid-term, Ms. Lee assigned Abiola a "mentor"—a fellow student who could help him navigate the school. Hoping to build a bridge between the African American and Nigerian students, she asked Warren, an African American student, to stay after class so she could introduce them formally.

It did not go as planned. "I didn't know you were asking me to stay after school for *this*," Warren said. "You know the other Nigerian kids have been calling us names like the n-word, right?" Abiola stood motionless, eyes cast downward.

"What?" Ms. Lee responded, puzzled. "Why? That doesn't make sense." she said.

"They think they're better than us," Warren explained. "They think they're not Black."

"I'm not 'Black,'" Abiola said defensively, "I'm Nigerian."

Ms. Lee replied, "Well all of you need to learn how to get along because I won't have this kind of conflict in my classroom. You just met!"

Later, after the school day ended, a small group of Nigerian students got into a shoving match with a small group of African American students in the parking lot. The melee was broken up before punches were thrown, but tensions remained high.

Speaking with a couple colleagues about the incident, Ms. Lee said, "I can't understand it. I know there are always social tensions with kids this age, but they're all Black. You would think they would get along better because they have that in common."

"Well I *do* understand it," replied Ms. Thompkins, one of the few African American teachers at the school. "Our school contributes to the tension by treating the students like they are the same when they don't see it that way."

Mr. Werth responded, "So you're saying *we're* the problem here? I always try to see what students have in common instead of their differences. They should do the same."

Ms. Lee knew she did not understand the complexities of the situation, but something about what Mr. Werth had just said did not feel right to her. She wished all her students would get along, but she also wondered what she could do differently to quell the tensions.

Questions

1 What factors should Ms. Lee have taken into consideration when choosing a mentor for Abiola?

2 What, if anything, should Ms. Lee have done differently to address Warren's concerns and to ensure that Abiola felt welcomed? What might the school administration do to address the growing conflict?

3 Mr. Werth expressed a color-blind mentality when he said he tries to only see commonalities among students. How might a color-blind approach affect his ability to understand and address the situation at hand?

CASE 11.3: A LEGACY OF PRIVILEGE ON THE SOCCER PITCH

The women's soccer team at Park Heights School had won several tournaments. Among the sports for which the school had both women's teams and men's teams, soccer was the only one for which women's games drew more spectators than men's games. Mr. Rosenthal, the long-time coach, was proud of the team's consistent success.

What had become less consistent, though, was the racial make-up of the team. The demographics of the school and team was changing as greater numbers of Mexican and Salvadoran families, mostly undocumented immigrants, moved into the area. At first the children of these families were hesitant to participate in school activities, so a local community organization started a youth soccer league. Little by little, the Mexican and Salvadoran young women were trying out for and making the Park Heights team.

The previous season, Mr. Rosenthal and Ms. Ferris, the principal, received several phone calls from white parents complaining about the roster. Several of these parents had supported the district's soccer program since their children were young and wanted the school to prioritize the "homegrown" students. Because this season was the first in which there was a real possibility the team would become majority Latina players, these parents grew increasingly protective. Their sentiment was supported by Save Park Heights, a local organization created to pressure local legislators into passing laws to deny undocumented immigrants access to public services. The girls' soccer team was used as an illustration of how, in their words, "real citizens are losing opportunities to illegals."

Ms. Ferris hated controversy, which worried Mr. Rosenthal when he learned a group of parents planned to meet with Ms. Ferris in person to discuss their complaints. "What do you plan to tell them?" he asked.

"I only plan on listening. Then we'll meet and I'll fill you in," she replied.

Later, when Mr. Rosenthal and Ms. Ferris met, she told him the parents threatened to work with Save Park Heights to direct negative press to the school if they didn't do something to "reverse the trend."

"What does that mean?" Mr. Rosenthal asked. "The players try out. We choose the best players. I'm not getting into politics. All I can do is choose the best players."

Ms. Ferris responded, "I hear you. On the other hand, if they intensify the controversy it could hurt *all* our immigrant students."

"What are you asking me to do?" Mr. Rosenthal inquired.

"Just try to keep things even," his principal replied.

"You mean, however tryouts go, make sure I don't give more than half the spots to Latina players? How do we explain that to *their* families?" Mr. Rosenthal asked.

Ms. Ferris said, "Do anything you can to avoid this controversy. As for the Latina families, they're not speaking up. All we can do is respond to people who speak up."

Suddenly Mr. Rosenthal was not looking forward to tryouts. He had his orders, but he knew they were unjust, for *all* the players.

Questions

1 How should Ms. Ferris have responded to parents of players who met with her to complain? Should Mr. Rosenthal follow her instructions even if he thinks they are unjust?

2 Why might the Mexican and Salvadoran families be hesitant to speak up about the controversy? Do you agree with Ms. Ferris's assessment that she should not consider their concerns because they were not speaking up?

3 Ms. Ferris was concerned about the potential impact on all immigrant families in the school, not just the Mexican and Salvadorian families. How might the Save Park Heights campaign already be impacting immigrant families in the community?

CASE 11.4: FAMILY INVOLVEMENT

Joel Pham's parents reliably attended conferences, but that was the extent of their involvement when it came to visiting Joel's school.

Joel's mother, Ms. Pham, worked for a local printing company known for encouraging employees to do community service. The company even paid employees to volunteer during designated work days throughout the year. Most employees whose children attended the school came to school on these days to assist teachers, but Ms. Pham never participated.

Like many teachers, Mr. Rolnick believed family involvement was integral to student success, so he constantly tried to provide opportunities for parents to volunteer, such as by shelving library books or updating bulletin boards. Understanding some people might want to be involved but have difficulty getting to the school, he also included work-from-home opportunities such as preparing materials for school events. Joel's parents never responded to these opportunities.

Mr. Rolnick was sensitive to parents who worked multiple jobs and could not afford to take time off work. He was bothered, though, that Joel's parents, who to his knowledge had no such limitations, showed no interest in being involved. Mr. Rolnick knew transportation was not an issue for them. The family lived in walking distance. He knew

Joel and his parents were ethnically Vietnamese, but Ms. and Mr. Pham were raised in the U.S., so language was not a barrier.

One day, Joel expressed interest in working with a classmate, Myles, for the Science Fair. Mr. Rolnick said he would need to speak to the parents first, since joint projects needed teacher and parent approval. He called Mr. Pham and suggested everyone meet to devise a plan that would ensure both boys had equal responsibilities. Mr. Rolnick explained to Mr. Pham that his schedule was flexible, but Mr. Pham said he would speak with Joel at home instead. Mr. Rolnick could not believe Mr. Pham's passivity when it came to his son's education.

He turned to a coworker for advice. Ms. Smith had taught in the school more than twenty-five years. "I've reached out to the Phams several times, but they just aren't involved," Mr. Rolnick complained.

"I don't want to speak for them," Ms. Smith said, "but I encourage you to think about other barriers. I remember Joel's parents. They attended this school when there were few Vietnamese families in the area. Unfortunately, the school was not welcoming. I'm sure they were happy to move on. Some of the same teachers are here— teachers who were not supportive of them. Perhaps that explains part of their reluctance."

"But I'm not one of those teachers," Mr. Rolnick said.

"You're not," Ms. Smith replied. "But is it possible that the assumptions you're making or the way you're approaching the Phams could remind them of some of those teachers?"

"Maybe you're right," Mr. Rolnick conceded, wondering what he could do to help Ms. and Mr. Pham feel welcome.

Questions

1   Mr. Rolnick provided various opportunities for students' parents to volunteer, but Ms. and Mr. Pham did not volunteer in these ways. Ms. Smith suggested that one reason for their lack of participation might be their own experience as students in the school. What other factors might be keeping them from volunteering?

2   How should Mr. Rolnick and other teachers and administrators reach out to parents and other caretakers who might have experienced school as a hostile environment when they were students? How would the staff even know this is a barrier?

3 Mr. Rolnick appeared to assume, because they didn't take advantage of family involvement opportunities he created, that Ms. and Mr. Pham were disinterested in their son's education. What are some ways parents can be involved and demonstrate interest in their children's education other than volunteering at the school?

CASE 11.5: MY UNCLE

Abdi was an energetic student who excelled academically. He was liked by peers, but their patience with him was diminishing because he often needed to be reminded to stop talking and pay attention. Ms. Klein, his teacher, had noticed his tendency to talk a lot and to be distracted even before the school year began, during a "Meet Your Teacher" event. Abdi's excitement for school was obvious, but despite instructions from his mother to wait his turn and listen to the teacher, he had difficulty following directions. It wasn't until his father sternly reprimanded him that evening that his behavior changed. Upon seeing this, Ms. Klein knew Abdi was *capable* of following rules, but that he needed guidance.

As she was planning for November conferences, Ms. Klein was sure to remind Abdi that his mother *and* father should attend. She wanted to discuss Abdi's behavior with his parents in person because she did not want them to misinterpret her concerns and think Abdi was being disrespectful. Instead, she wanted them to understand he simply struggled to stop talking when he should be listening, becoming a distraction for other students. From what she observed at the Meet Your Teacher event, she hoped Adbi's father would address the behavior concerns effectively.

When Abdi's designated conference time arrived, his mother, Ms. Asha, entered Ms. Klein's classroom with a man who introduced himself as Abdi's uncle. After hearing Ms. Klein's concerns, they agreed to speak to Abdi about his conduct. Ms. Klein, skeptical that this would resolve the issue, suggested they inform Abdi's father on the issue. They promised to convey the information, but Ms. Klein worried they were saying so only to appease her.

After saying goodbye to Abdi's mother and uncle, Ms. Klein went to the main office to check her mailbox. "You look frustrated," the office administrator, Ms. Larson, observed.

"I *am* frustrated," Ms. Klein replied. She scanned the office to make sure nobody was around. "I just finished Abdi's conference. I was hoping to speak with his father about Abdi's behavior, but he didn't come. Abdi's mother and someone who said he was Abdi's uncle came. I don't have much confidence either will be able to influence Abdi to behave better in class. Abdi's so bright. He just needs guidance."

"Abdi is a sweet kid," Ms. Larson said. "As for the uncle, I've seen several people over the years arrive after school to pick Abdi up claiming to be his uncle. To be honest, I don't think any of them are related. I've seen the same thing with other immigrant students."

Shaking her head in disbelief, Ms. Klein said, "I'll keep you posted if I learn anything."

The next day Ms. Klein noticed Abdi was his usual talkative self. She approached him and said, "I had a good conference with your mom and uncle yesterday."

Abdi smiled and said, "That's what my mom said, too."

"That's great!" Ms. Klein replied. "It was nice for your uncle to come, too. Is he your mom's brother or your dad's brother?"

Abdi, puzzled and embarrassed, responded, "Neither."

Ms. Klein sighed and thought, *I'll have to let Ms. Larson know she was right.*

Questions

1 Based on Ms. Klein's observations, was Abdi's father's presence at conferences necessary? What are some reasons somebody else from the family might attend meetings at the school in his place?

2 How might Ms. Larson's distrust of certain visitors affect how she interacts with them?

3 Ms. Klein asked Abdi about his relationship with his uncle to gather more information regarding who attended the meeting with his mother. Based on Abdi's response, how might that exchange impact his comfort level in the classroom and his relationship with Ms. Klein?

Appendix A

The Equity Literacy Case Analysis Worksheet

Step 1: Identify biases or inequities.

Step 2: Take stock of various perspectives.

Step 3: Consider possible challenges and opportunities.

Step 4: Imagine equitable and just outcomes.

Step 5: Brainstorm immediate-term solutions.

Step 6: Brainstorm long-term solutions.

Step 7: Craft a plan of action.

APPENDIX B

POINTS FOR CONSIDERATION

Case 3.1: Chocolate Bar Fundraiser

- As a form of decision-making, voting captures the majority desire but does not always result in an equitable decision. Sometimes we must support an unpopular course of action because it's the just thing to do, even if most people disagree with it.
- This case provides an important opportunity to discuss how PTA meetings and other opportunities for in-school family involvement are often not as accessible to economically marginalized families as they are to wealthier families. Parents experiencing poverty are more likely than their wealthier peers to work multiple jobs without paid leave, including evening jobs, and are less likely to be able to afford childcare or public transportation if necessary to participate. So, although it can be easy to interpret lower levels of some types of school involvement by low-income families as an indication that they don't value education, we might ask ourselves, instead, how we might make opportunities for school involvement more accessible to families experiencing poverty.
- Mr. Winterstein illustrates what often is called "deficit ideology," suggesting that lower-income kids could sell just as many chocolate bars as their peers if they worked harder. The problem with the deficit view is that it ignores context, like the inability for economically marginalized families to afford a large percentage of their children's chocolate bar allotment. Being an equitable and just educator means, in part, being able to recognize the

deficit view and refusing to contribute to it by blaming youth experiencing poverty for the results of their poverty.

- Parent groups such as the PTA play an important role in schools. Although some PTAs are viewed simply as a mechanism for bringing volunteers to schools or to fundraise, it is important to realize the collective power these groups can have. They can make a significant impact by contacting local elected officials such as school board members, mayors, and state representatives and expressing their concerns over school funding and other issues. Setting aside time in meetings to learn about advocacy and changes in funding or policy can help the groups be more effective when making decisions and affecting more substantial change.

Case 3.2: The Trouble with Grit

- Despite its growing popularity, the "grit" framework can be understood as another in a long history of strategies and initiatives that help us avoid naming and addressing educational injustice. The problems with "grit" are plenty, but two are particularly salient to this case. Firstly, the most marginalized students, including students experiencing poverty, already are the grittiest students. They must overcome far more barriers and challenges than students with more access to economic and other kinds of privilege—barriers and challenges they never should have to face. They are the *models* of grit. Secondly, we must be careful not to reactively define educational outcome disparities (like test scores or homework grades) as a lack of grit or as deficient mindsets while we refuse to attend to those barriers and challenges. Grit is not a path to equity and justice because it fails to account for inequity and injustice.
- As equity literate educators, we should learn to resist the impulse to adopt a deficit view of families like Samantha's. We can practice adopting a *structural view* instead. A structural view challenges us to consider, first, the structural challenges and barriers that impede student performance and growth. In Samantha's case, these might be big-level structural conditions like poverty itself, economic justice issues that cause and sustain poverty like the scarcity of living wage

work and how those issues affect families and their engagement in school, or biases and inequities in school policies and practices. It also challenges us to consider how the policies and practices we and our schools adopt might disadvantage some students and privilege others. When we form the habit of foregrounding these concerns, we position ourselves to be a threat to inequity.

- Samantha's mother is working multiple jobs. She is doing what she needs to do, given the scarcity of living wage work in the U.S., to provide for her family. Samantha is spending her afternoons and evenings caring for younger siblings, feeding them, and helping them with homework. As educators, perhaps we are not in a position to secure every family living wage work or other resources and opportunities—preventive healthcare, stable affordable housing— that would bolster the educational success of students experiencing poverty. But we can shift policy and practice to be responsive to these barriers. Sometimes policy and practice designed with the "median" family in mind punish the most marginalized families for the implications of the ways they are already marginalized.

Case 3.3: Student Protest

- Students who are denied equitable educational opportunity often are very attuned to the inequities they are experiencing. It is only natural that they would look for ways to respond. Unfortunately, when youth who experience injustice respond, even in the most peaceful and constructive ways, they often are viewed as trouble-makers. This case provides an important opportunity to reflect on the subtle and not-so-subtle ways students might be seen as troublemakers simply for advocating for educational equity.
- Walkouts are a common form of student protest. School administrators and local law enforcement officials often respond to student walkout plans by increasing police presence in schools. By doing so they might increase tensions in the short term and criminalize student self-efficacy in the long term.
- School closings tend to take place in neighborhoods already blighted by other challenges, including declining infrastructure, high foreclosure rates, and a lack of services such as banks and

hospitals. Declining enrollment often occurs because of these external factors. It is important to consider these institutional factors that lead to school closures and attempt to address them proactively rather than reactively.

Case 3.4: High Expectations or Unrealistic Goals?

- This case showcases the reality that access and opportunity often are granted on the basis of existing levels of access and opportunity. As educators who are committed to providing students with equitable access, it is worthwhile to consider what institutional factors in our schools and districts prohibit students from reaching their goals, including having access to higher education options upon completing high school.
- Although Ms. Sutter recognized Mr. Stein's comments as prejudicial, she did not have the same reaction when her peers said similar things during the staff meeting. Their comments might not have been as blatant as Mr. Stein's, but it is important to note that they were all biased. These types of negative assumptions, subtle or not, have the potential to influence how teachers approach daily instruction and interaction with students. Research shows that teachers' expectations for students influence student outcomes tremendously. Consider what disservice and harm we do when we try to limit students by what we or society thinks is realistic for them.
- Clearly students' families were interested in supporting the club Ms. Sutter created. Knowing this, Ms. Sutter might have collaborated with these families to co-design the program, drawing on the conversations about college some of them already might have been having at home.
- It is important to remember to present higher education as a series of options, careful to encourage students to think about those options without disparaging people who did not go to college or who are choosing presently not to pursue higher education. When we disparage people who do not pursue higher education, we are indirectly disparaging the families of students who could become the first people in their families to attend college.

Case 3.5: Technology Progress, Equity Regress

- Sometimes what might look like technological progress can create or deepen inequities if not implemented with the needs and access of the most economically marginalized families in mind. We should prepare all students with technology literacy. However, we should do so without potentially punishing those who cannot afford computers or Internet access at home.

- Students experiencing poverty are less likely to have transportation to or from a library or their school if they need to arrive early or stay late to use a computer. They might also be working or caring for younger siblings after school. These are not reasonable alternatives for students who do not have access to computer or Internet technologies at home. Neither is expecting people who can least afford big data plans for their cell phones to access the Internet on their phones a reasonable alternative.

- Too often the educators most outspoken and courageous on matters of diversity and social justice are marginalized in their school communities, labeled as troublemakers like Ms. Dehne. In a school committed to equity, educators with the most understanding and passion for diversity and social justice should constitute the core of the institutional culture. This case provides an important opportunity to discuss why people like Ms. Dehne are sometimes labeled as troublemakers for making a point every educator should have the equity literacy to make. Sometimes creating change is about speaking out, while other times it's about supporting others who are speaking out.

Case 4.1: The Winter Party

- It is important to distinguish between inclusivity and tokenism. Focusing primarily on Christmas-themed activities and then including a Hanukkah activity and a Kwanzaa activity is tokenism. Hanukkah, after all, traditionally, is not a major Jewish holiday in the way Christmas is a major Christian holiday. Notice, too, that the people who are planning this event never explicitly raised a question about what such a party would mean for students who do not celebrate Kwanzaa, Hanukkah, or Christmas, including students from a variety of religious and spiritual traditions that do not celebrate holidays at all or students whose families do not practice any religion.

- Kwanzaa is not a religious holiday, but rather a celebration of African heritage and African American culture. Several misperceptions about this and other non-Christian holidays are perpetuated in schools. If we are going to discuss holidays at all, we should ensure we are prepared to discuss all of them without perpetuating these misperceptions.

- Although Ms. Tate is happy that volunteers are taking ownership of the party, it is important to note that teachers are ultimately responsible for what happens in their classrooms. Sometimes a democratic vote doesn't land on the most equitable decision. While it may be easier for an educator to allow the "majority rules" parents to do some heavy lifting in the classroom or school, this often marginalizes parents with other views or experiences, whose numbers are fewer, or who might not be able to be present to represent their viewpoints. Wealth and privilege are also operating here. Asserting that something is "no big deal" is an act that privileged-identity people can use to assert privilege and silence dissent, so that speaking up becomes inherently "a big deal."

- This case provides an important opportunity to discuss the variety of ways Christianity is privileged in public schools. Although many public schools have become more conscious of not explicitly celebrating Christian holidays while ignoring or tokenizing those from other traditions, there are many ways Christianity continues to be normalized in public schools. The simplest example might be the fact that "winter break" is scheduled around Christmas and "spring break" is often scheduled around Easter. Ms. Tyler's comment that Christmas is not religious, but American, is evidence of this normalization.

Case 4.2: Christmas Lights?

- Because of Ms. Bren's own cultural view, she assumed the lights she saw were Christmas lights, not decorative lights. Around October and November, some religious holidays such as Diwali,

the Hindu festival of lights, or Eid-al-Fitr, the celebration mark-
ing the end of Ramadan for Muslims, might occur. People from
these faiths, as well as others, may use strings of lights as decora-
tions for religious festivals.

- Ms. Bren's students who were bothered by her Tweet and
her conversation with her colleague did not feel comfortable
expressing why they were bothered. If students feel disengaged
or disrespected, even the best pedagogical strategies or lesson
plans can be ineffective. The danger then becomes attributing
student performance in class to their abilities or desires to learn,
rather than examining the environment created by the teacher
that caused students to disengage.

- As educators, we should remember that students constantly eval-
uate our actions during the school day, at school functions, and
on social media. What is overheard between teachers or communicated through social media can have just as much impact
as what students hear from us in the classroom. For this reason,
it is critical to foster a classroom environment in which students
can question or challenge a teacher or their peers without fearing
negative repercussions.

Case 4.3: A Difference in Perspectives

- Mr. Ortiz was hesitant to educate members of the school
community, including students in his class, about the positive
significance of the symbol, perhaps because of his lack of famil-
iarity with it. However, by not addressing the situation more
thoughtfully, he could be depriving students of a valuable lesson in critical thinking. As Madelyn demonstrated, students are
eager to learn things that challenge their views and to share that
knowledge with others.

- Mr. Ortiz told Nikhil he should not wear the charm at school
because of its potential to disrupt other students. Legal prec-
edents suggest that school officials *can* censor religious and
political expression if they can demonstrate or reasonably fore-
cast that the expression will cause a *substantial* disruption in the
school. This case provides an important opportunity to explore

what constitutes a substantial disruption and how interpretations of "disruption" might change depending upon whose cultural symbols are at issue.

- There have been numerous cases in the U.S. of students being asked to remove religious symbols or articles of clothing in schools because of dress code violations. Community reaction to these interventions has varied considerably from situations involving rosary beads to those involving hijabs. Educators might be inclined to appeal to the majority voice, or to what they *believe* most people think. While this approach may seem sensible, it is rarely equitable. When we make decisions on the basis of appeasing the majority we risk marginalizing people who, like Nikhil, are not in the majority.

Case 4.4: Islamophobic Read-Aloud

- Being equitable educators requires us to take a stand on issues like Islamophobia when they arise in class. If we don't take a stand, even if we try to appear neutral, it can look to students as though we are complying with the dominant or discriminatory view. In many ways, *not responding* is just as much a response as *responding*.
- This case provides an opportunity to discuss how important it is to be mindful of who our students are and how power is distributed among them. In this case, knowing George's reputation and the heaviness of the topic, Ms. McGrath might have been better off collecting the free writes and then picking one or two of them to share.
- Notice George's collective language—his use of "we" and "us." Work on learning how to catch these subtle declarations of community agreement and to analyze who they really include. Obviously in this case they do not include Hasina or Essam, and they probably don't include many other students in the room, so the very language in George's free write implicitly sets up an "us/them" dichotomy that cements their identities as "outsiders." We should be mindful of whether we are contributing to similar types of insider/outsider dichotomies in the language we use.

Case 5.1: Protesting the Pledge

- Given time constraints and other challenges, it can be difficult to know when to detour from a planned lesson to address a current event or to give students space to discuss a controversial topic. Choosing not to respond at all, however, can suggest agreement with the sentiment that is being expressed. If a student is being silenced or criticized for peacefully taking an equity stand, we should commit to taking a detour from the planned lesson to address it.

- Even if school or district policy states that students can abstain from reciting the Pledge or national anthem, it's important to be mindful of whether the classroom climate allows for students to not participate. A negative social consequence, as Kate is experiencing, or perhaps even backlash from staff can implicitly coerce participation.

- Even if you consider the Pledge or anthem to be sacred, as many people do, it's important to understand that some people might protest because they see a gap between the promises of rights symbolized by the Pledge and anthem and the present reality of inequity.

- Mr. Harrold could ask students if they can think of other examples from U.S. history when people were criticized for protesting on behalf of social justice causes and how perceptions of those people and the criticism they faced changed over time. Why is there a tendency in the U.S. for many people to be more upset about protests than about the conditions being protested?

Case 5.2: Not Time for Stories

- Because Ms. Ward dismissed DeQuan's contribution as a *story* rather than an *answer* to her question, he and other students might feel their contributions are not valued. Storytelling is a rich tradition in many families and might be a natural part of communication for some students. In some ways his ability to make connections between various events and topics demonstrates a more advanced cognitive process than the kind for which Ms. Ward was asking. She could have seen in DeQuan's story descriptive words about California, such as "sunny" and "warm." These were the same words she recorded after hearing them from Maddy.

- Ms. Ward validated Maddy's contribution by saying she was correct, perhaps indirectly communicating to DeQuan that he was incorrect. Ms. Ward also distanced herself from DeQuan by telling him he was being disrespectful when he might have thought *she* was being disrespectful by interrupting him. This provides an opportunity to discuss ways students' behaviors can be as much a reflection of our own missteps as it is about them, and the humility it takes to consider this possibility.

- Ms. Ward's initial question limited responses to students who had traveled to California, which would have excluded, and might have alienated, students whose families could not afford such a trip.

- Attempting to proactively avoid further "disruption" from DeQuan, Ms. Ward called out his potential behavior in front of class, further embarrassing him. It is worthwhile to consider the long-term effects of these sorts of microaggressions on student engagement when they happen repeatedly over time. Furthermore, if Ms. Ward incorrectly views DeQuan's behavior as disrespectful, and this type of interaction between the two of them continues, DeQuan runs the risk of having a negative reputation follow him in subsequent years, compounding the bias.

Case 5.3: Teaching Thanksgiving

- While most (although not all) schools no longer rely on overt, stereotypical teachings of "Pilgrims and Indians" during Thanksgiving, these teachings remain prevalent in many parts of U.S. culture. Students see images in media and advertising. They hear misinformation from family and friends who hold onto inaccurate stories. By addressing this misinformation or lack of information, we can take advantage of opportunities to teach critical thinking. For example, the histories and perspectives of Indigenous people are often omitted from curricula, so holidays such as Columbus Day and Thanksgiving provide opportunities to initiate a kind of critical learning that can be applied to a variety of topics throughout the school year.

- It can be powerful, for example, to explore with students why Thanksgiving or Columbus Day are observed by many Indigenous people as a day of mourning. Regardless of the racial composition of students, we should address this perspective and its history. The term "Happy Thanksgiving" does not resonate with everyone because it obscures significant historical events that continue to impact American Indians today. By not discussing multiple viewpoints about Thanksgiving, and simply focusing on other aspects such as food or thankfulness, we perpetuate misinformation and a larger U.S. mythology that buries histories of oppression under celebrations.

- The burden of changing inequitable teaching practices often falls on those who have the insights and will to raise concerns about existing inequitable practices. Although we certainly want people with the deepest knowledge about equity to participate in equity efforts, we should be careful not to place the responsibility to raise these concerns fully on one or two people. Doing so might become a deterrent for those who wish to challenge existing conditions. Also, studies have shown in particular that teachers of color often bear extra uncompensated responsibilities for doing "diversity and inclusion" work in schools because people assume they have the expertise and interest to do it.

- As educators we all should feel a sense of urgency to respond to and redress inequity in our schools despite time constraints and to support one another when teachable moments occur.

Case 5.4: Multicultural Day Parade

- Ms. Morrison used the words "ethnic" and "cultural" interchangeably when describing the type of clothing that would be showcased in the parade. Typically, *ethnicity* is used to describe a person's ancestral, geographical background while *culture* is used to describe the norms of a group that could include people from various ethnicities. Additionally, *nationality* refers to the country of citizenship (which is not something everybody has in an

official sense) while *race* generally refers to groups of people identified by skin color and other attributes. It is important to note
that each of these concepts is, to one extent or another, *socially
constructed*. That is, they are classification systems designed by
humans rather than scientifically based. (This is why, for example, a Colombian citizen can be considered white in Colombia
but Latinx in the United States.)

- Many schools host a Diversity or Multicultural Day instead of
integrating diversity and equity in deeper ways or instead of
addressing inequities at all. Sometimes, in these sorts of events,
students who feel alienated because of the way they are treated
based on their identities throughout the year are asked to showcase their differences from the cultural "norm," which could
further alienate them from their peers. It is not equitable to
request that students who feel marginalized participate in these
events while the conditions that marginalize them still exist. The
time and resources given to celebratory events is justified if com-
parable attention is given to addressing inequities in schools.

- Ms. Morrison described the special clothing as "costumes,"
which is a word many people associate with Halloween or make-
believe play clothes. Use of the word to describe clothing youth
associate with their heritage could trivialize their cultures.

- Ms. Morrison had clear expectations for what she considered
parade-worthy clothing. She assumed students would understand the notion of ethnic heritage and act accordingly. Once
she realized otherwise, as with Keisha and Emily, she asserted
her judgment and failed to see how their definition of "cultural
clothing" was different from hers. Notice that Keisha was dismissed without consideration of the possibility that she, as an
African American, might not have been able to trace her heritage
to somewhere outside the United States or have access to clothing that she identified as representing her ethnic background.
Similarly, Emily may not know her ethnic background or have
resources to acquire clothing for the event. Other students in
class who are descendants of slaves or who were adopted might
not know what their ethnic heritage is. Ms. Morrison failed to
capture the opportunity to learn more about how her students
and their families self-identify.

Case 5.5: A Place to Study

- This case reflects the importance of considering impact rather than intent. Ms. Grady intends to help her students become better learners. However, the impact of her actions might create barriers to their learning. A quiet and isolated space might not be available in all students' homes. Moreover, a collective approach might be more valued by the family over quiet isolation, in which case the pencil case could be used by everyone in the household. Ms. Grady might have been setting Shua up to create conflict in his family by expecting him to tell his siblings they were not allowed to use his resources.

- Note that the scenario does not indicate whether Shua's homework situation negatively affected his academic success. This lack of indication raises questions about the appropriateness of discussing it at a conference when doing so might create distance between the family and teacher. Additionally, Ms. Grady assumed Shua's parents would not follow through on providing additional learning support at home. This assumption could impact how she engages them during the conference. Ms. Grady's good intentions could have a negative impact on her relationship with Shua and his family.

- Ms. Grady is worried about whether Shua is completing homework by himself. Would she harbor the same concern for a student who turned in homework without food stains or items crossed out? Is it possible that Shua's brother is helping him, *perhaps even teaching* him, which is a good outcome?

Case 6.1: Black Lives Matter

- When conversations about racism and other social justice issues happen in school, they often are paced with the safety and comfort of the most resistant students and families in mind. While we do want to consider how to build bridges for all learners, we should be careful not to prioritize the short-term safety and comfort of racially or otherwise privileged students or colleagues over our commitment to equity and justice, or over the long-term safety and comfort of students or colleagues who are being marginalized.

- There has never been an ideology or message attached to the BLM movement that suggests Black lives are the *only* lives that matter. The guiding principles of the BLM movement explicitly state, "To love and desire freedom and justice for ourselves is a necessary prerequisite for wanting the same for others." In fact, the BLM movement is perhaps the most inclusive, intersectional movement in the history of U.S. social movements. By responding to BLM by arguing *all lives matter*, we strip the commitment to racial justice for African Americans out of the messaging. When we do so we cheat *all* students out of an opportunity for authentic learning about racism. We also reinforce a dangerous color-blind ideology that sacrifices deep understandings of racial justice for shallow and false notions of racial harmony. (For more information about the guiding principles of the BLM movement, visit http://blacklivesmatter.com/guiding-principles/.)

- Some students might not have many opportunities at home to consider community issues through a social justice lens, either because their racial privilege protects them from the need to have these opportunities or because their parents do not engage them in these conversations. Ms. Simmons demonstrated equity literacy in wanting to capture this teachable moment for students as well as providing students whose communities are the targets of racism with a chance to share their insights. It's important to have strategies for addressing these issues, such as the tensions between "Black Lives Matter" and "All Lives Matter." For example, one way to promote critical thinking could be to draw parallels with other campaigns, such as the Start Seeing Motorcycles campaign, which is a national campaign created to raise awareness of motorcycle related traffic accidents. Why is there not a similar Start Seeing Cars campaign? This conversation might provide a bridge for students to understand the marginalization of suggesting All Lives Matter while lending support to the experiences of marginalized students.

Case 6.2: Teaching Race with *Huckleberry Finn*

- Because Samuel was the only student in Ms. Kohl's class who responded publicly to the language in *Huck Finn*, it might be easy to assume he was the only student upset by it. Remember, though, that students choose not to speak up for a variety of reasons. Some may remain silent in the face of painful bias or oppression because they know there is a social price to pay for speaking up or because they believe they will not be heard if they do speak up.

- Although Samuel's conduct and language were disruptive to the lesson, we should consider the circumstances that led to his reaction. Samuel displayed signs of discomfort with what he might have perceived as a hostile environment, but Ms. Kohl continued the activity. Punishing Samuel for his actions could send the message that he was not allowed to feel how he did and that Ms. Kohl's actions were acceptable because she was in a position of authority.

- Words are powerful—especially words, like the n-word, with oppressive histories. It is a luxury of white privilege to see that word in a piece of literature and think of it solely as a marker of a historical context. Unfortunately, people who have been targeted with the word do not have that luxury, so we should carefully consider how, or *whether*, we want to allow the n-word or similarly derogatory terms in any aspect of our classrooms. Certainly, if we do choose to read literature containing such language, we must prepare ourselves and students for it and discuss its racist roots.

- Too often when students learn about racism in school, they learn about it solely in the past tense, perhaps through novels like *Huck Finn* or *To Kill a Mockingbird*. Racism remains relevant today but often is not discussed in schools in the present tense, even when teachable moments occur. Help students make that connection to avoid contributing to the perception that racism was solved with the Civil Rights Movement.

Case 6.3: Diverse Friends Day

- It is important to acknowledge that Mr. Carbondale has good intentions; he sees himself as an advocate for students and demonstrates enthusiasm about the growing diversity in his school.

It is equally important, though, to distinguish between appreciating diversity and advocating for equity and justice. Events such as Diverse Friends Day are about the former, about racial *harmony*, but they are not necessarily about racial *justice*. They do not address underlying racial tensions or inequities, which is why some students of color might be uncomfortable with them. We should examine the amount of time and resources allocated to celebrating diversity as compared with the time and resources devoted to building equitable and just classrooms and schools.

- This case provides an opportunity to discuss the ways marginalized students, including students of color, often are put in positions to have to do the diversity educating. In this case, students of color are being asked to make themselves more vulnerable than some of them already feel at Lozen School. When we use activities such as Diverse Friends Day, we might be assuming students enter the experience equally, on a level playing field. Usually this is a bad assumption, which is part of what the students are explaining to Mr. Carbondale.

- Mr. Carbondale could not have known the full community's attitudes about this type of an event, perhaps because of the effects of his own racial privilege, unless he solicited opinions from a diverse group of people, not just his principal. People who are involved with this type of decision-making always should elicit feedback from a diversity of people—including people who will be most greatly affected by the decision—before proceeding.

- Many, perhaps *most*, "diversity" initiatives encourage some level of cultural sharing but fall short of creating more equitable environments for marginalized students. When not carried out in conjunction with attention to racial or other inequities, these initiatives can contribute to the very conditions they are being designed, ostensibly, to counteract.

Case 6.4: Terms of Endearment

- Even if—and this is a very big *if*—Reggie sincerely wasn't offended by Anthony's use of the term, it was very likely that other students, such as Keisha, *were* offended, including students who were not African American. Failing to address the name calling could send a message to students that it's ok to use racist language in class.

- Reggie's discomfort as Ms. Lawson prodded him might suggest that he really *wasn't* fine with Anthony using the n-word. In some social contexts, people who are the targets of oppressive language, whether people using that language intend to be offensive or not, might feel at least temporarily pressured to pretend they are not offended, knowing there is a social price to pay for speaking up.

- There also might be cases in which students, hearing words such as the n-word used in popular culture, are not completely attuned to the words' histories or even their full contemporary implications. We should prepare to help students learn about the power of these words by informing ourselves about them, from variations on the n-word to "retard" or "that's so gay."

- Ms. Lawson felt prepared to take instructional advantage of the diversity in her school, but she was not prepared to facilitate difficult conversations, such as one about the n-word. As educators, we must equip ourselves with strategies for engaging students in conversations about these issues because not doing so could suggest we condone bias or injustice.

Case 6.5: An Uncomfortable Field Trip

- It can be easy when we observe students behaving in ways we interpret as inappropriate to find fault with them without wondering whether we have created the conditions for their behavior. By joking and laughing, Kevin and Hakeem might have been masking their discomfort or finding a small measure of safety with one another in an uncomfortable setting. Back in the classroom, their peers also made light of the field trip. Perhaps there was something about their experience at the agency, including noticing the lack of diversity there, that made them question the suggestion that with hard work and good grades they too could work there. It's important to have the humility to consider how students might experience a learning activity differently from how we intend it.

- Although Ms. Anderson felt the experience was a failure and blamed this failure at least in part on the fact that she tried to do it with "the wrong students," the day might have gone better with fairly simple adjustments. For example, Ms. Anderson could have prepared her students for the lack of diversity they could encounter at the agency and encouraged open conversation about it.
- One stressor on students revolves around attire, especially if their families don't have sufficient resources to purchase a large selection of clothing. As educators, we must avoid perpetuating this stressor, especially by connecting it to a school activity.

Case 6.6: Build the Wall

- Social justice and equity are not spectator sports, neither are they limited to the school day. We need to be prepared so we will know how to respond to instances of bias and injustice at *all* times, especially in a school with a history of racist and xenophobic student behavior.
- We should engage people who are being marginalized into conversations about how to productively address how they are being treated. Similarly, it is important to educate the people doing the marginalizing and to hold them accountable. However, sometimes an immediate, assertive response is needed from somebody who has the power to provide that response. Maybe in this case that means the coach should end the game by walking off the court, or another school leader should chastise the behavior over the intercom system. It is important to not put students who are being pummeled with oppression in a position to feel they have to respond because nobody else is responding.
- Several organizations that track bullying, discrimination, and bias in schools reported increased incidents following President Trump's election. We might imagine schools, especially those in which we work, as exceptional, but no school is immune from the sociopolitical conditions around it. These conditions can interfere with students' engagement in school, so it is important to address them even if they do not happen in the classroom. Choosing not to respond can suggest agreement with the sentiment that is being expressed.

Case 7.1: Boys vs. Girls Trivia Contest

- It's always good to use a variety of teaching strategies to engage students and to involve them in decision-making. However, we also have an obligation to ensure that classrooms and schools are free of bias. In this particular case, Bill demonstrated subtle bias, such as addressing the class as "guys," and not-so-subtle bias, such as allowing disparaging remarks. His good intentions did not make his actions any less biased. This is why it is important to reflect on the biases we carry into the classroom and how these biases are communicated to students.

- Bill addressed disparaging remarks only as a disruption to the game rather than as gender bias. In doing so he missed an opportunity to help students understand that sexism has harmful personal and social consequences. Also, perhaps unintentionally, he condoned the behavior by not addressing it.

- Gender is not a "girl" and "boy" binary. Many individuals experience identities that do not fit so easily into these boxes. Some identify as transgender or genderqueer. Some youth might be unsure about their gender identities. This is one reason allowing the joking can be harmful even if we think it is good-natured. It puts young people who do not fit into simplistic categories in a position to feel like they have to play along with the jokes even if they feel targeted by them or choose to identify among options that may not reflect their identities. It's also important to be proactive about creating a bias-free environment for all students instead of waiting until a situation requires it.

Case 7.2: Gendered Bathrooms

- The comfort of people who are resistant to movement toward equity and justice never should be prioritized over the goals of equity and justice. In this case, people with significant institutional power sacrificed progress toward justice (as incomplete as that progress might be) to appease those who complained. This speaks to the *will* of equity literacy: being willing to withstand complaints and controversy and still doing the right thing.

- As educators committed to equity and justice, it is our responsibility to strengthen our equity literacy related to all ways students experience bias and injustice. There are many ways we can do this, from reading to attending local conferences to linking with networks of teachers who are working on social justice issues in schools (such as the New York Collective of Racial Educators, Teachers for Social Justice, or local chapters of the National Association for Multicultural Education). Strengthening our equity literacy can help us move from finding simple solutions to student concerns (a bathroom for Teryn to use), to equitable solutions (a bathroom Teryn can access).

- Too often conversations about injustice or bias are simplified into narrow concerns that are certainly important, but that also can obscure the bigger picture. This can happen when media focus narrowly on specific aspects of a bigger issue, especially if it garners a sudden rush of legal attention. In the case of transphobia in schools, this important but narrow focus has at times revolved around gender identity and bathrooms. It is important to understand this issue and its impact on transgender students, but it's also important to understand and consider the insights this issue can provide into the larger scope of transphobia. In equity literacy terms, this helps us transition from *responding* to bias and injustice to *redressing* bias and injustice.

Case 7.3: Timmy's Gender Nonconformity

- It can be easy for those of us who have not felt the sting of prejudice or oppression to believe young children are not ready to have conversations about issues like gender identity, race, or class. However, if prejudice and discrimination are present, it's our best evidence that youth, whatever age they might be, already are thinking about and trying to process these issues. If Ms. Grover fails to address this issue directly, she cheats students out of an opportunity to develop a deeper understanding of their own and others' identities and experiences. Another risk of not intervening in a direct way is that the failure to do so could implicitly send the message to Timmy and students who may not identify with a gender binary—who may not identify with stereotypical gender labels—that they are not welcome in Ms. Grover's classroom.

- Some students in this case were assuming the role of "gender police," policing one another into gender conformity through peer pressure. A failure to notice and address these early forms of policing could result in Timmy's internalization of the pressure to conform and to heightened policing by the students.
- Timmy's teachers tended to see students' treatment of him as teasing or bullying. Remember that teasing and bullying often are rooted in other issues related to institutional culture. Those underlying issues cannot be addressed only by interrupting the teasing or bullying, which are symptoms of the institutional culture. In order to address the issues in this case in the longer term, Ms. Grover will need to ask herself what it is about her classroom culture, or the school culture, or the broader societal culture that encourages or rewards the type of teasing and bullying Timmy was experiencing.

Case 7.4: Online Objectification

- Students who are bullied or harassed often are reluctant to report it for fear that the social cost of doing so will exceed the pain associated with the bullying or harassment. Similarly, students might be reluctant to stand up for others who are being discriminated against, bullied, or harassed because they worry about the social cost. This is why schools must have robust and comprehensive anti-discrimination, anti-bullying, and anti-bias policies and programs that are proactive rather than reactive, and for students to learn about and discuss these policies.
- On a similar note, youth who are being judged negatively for any reason might worry about seeming weak-minded if they speak up. They might worry they could be targeted in an intensified way for speaking up. This, again, is why we must learn how to recognize symptoms of bullying, harassment, and discrimination, and then learn how to address the issues underlying them rather than only responding to individual incidents.
- It can be easy to imagine a situation like this as a simple matter of Tyler making a bad choice. However, there are deeper issues

here that need to be uncovered and addressed if the goal is to create and sustain an equitable and just classroom and school. For example, heterosexual cis-gender young men often participate in these behaviors to assert or perform their masculinity. It also can be understood as a sense of entitlement to and need for control, which is at the root of much sexual harassment. Unfortunately, when schools attempt to address issues like online harassment, they often treat symptoms as "inappropriate behavior" without considering these underlying dynamics.

Case 7.5: Dress Code Distress

- This case presents an opportunity to consider the potential harm dress codes and other policies create when they do not account for diversity in body type, size, gender, gender-identity (as in restrictions on make-up use), ethnicity (restrictions on hair styles), household income (as in requiring uniforms or other new clothes), religion (as in restrictions on headwear), and other ways in which students identify.
- Some dress code policies can contribute to the sexualization or objectification of girls or young women by labeling types of clothing distracting to boys. This view conveys the message that young women are responsible for young men's reactions to them. This premise is not only sexist, but also heterosexist. Dress code guidelines also provide opportunities for students to be judgmental of one another, which could have negative self-esteem and body perception implications.
- Dress code enforcement presents a multitude of problems as well. In addition to being arbitrary and inconsistent, sometimes even targeting certain demographics, power dynamics might come into play when male teachers police female clothing, when female teachers police male clothing, or when any teacher polices the clothing of students who do not identify with the gender binary.

Case 8.1: A "Surprise" Fire Drill

- A high-pitched, intermittent blast along with the chaos that may ensue from a fire drill can be traumatic for some students on the Autism Spectrum. For some, the effects can last for days or weeks and compromise their abilities to function in the classroom. It's important to note that a student's ability to do well in a mainstream classroom is not an indicator of how severe they might react to particular stimuli or events, and this reaction itself might cause confusion with other students. There are many strategies to avoid this sort of trauma including, in this case, noise-reducing headphones.

- This case provides an interesting opportunity to consider the relationship between practicing *equality*, wherein all students are treated the same, and practicing *equity*, wherein all students are provided the supports they need to give them the best opportunity to succeed. Ms. Foster was concerned about creating an environment in which all her students, including Aiden, were given an equal opportunity to respond to the surprise fire drill. While her intentions were good, the impact of her desire to remove him from the classroom or deny him the headphones could be harmful.

- Keep in mind that, as educators, we should be advocates for our students, especially those from historically marginalized groups. Especially because Ms. Stintson was tasked by the principal to prepare her students, she should notify him of the barriers she is facing.

Case 8.2: Insufficient Accommodations

- This case points to tension between *equality* and *equity*. All students are invited on the same field trip, which would constitute a sort of equality. But once on the field trip not all students have the same access to learning opportunities, an obvious inequity. The best "accommodations" should provide equitable experiences rather than roughly equal experiences.

- Making choices for equity can be difficult. Often there is a lot to consider, including what Sonia Nieto has called the "sociopolitical context of schooling." It might be tempting to look at this one event and think, "It's just one field trip so it's no big deal if Justin is separated from the class while everybody else hikes."

But if we step back and consider the situation more broadly, we begin to see that students like Justin often experience little sleights, little fragments of inequity, that taken together could constitute a bigger inequitable school experience. Equity literacy means learning how to consider these single events in their larger contexts.

- Ms. Thurston might feel compelled to address this issue with Justin and Ms. Parsons exclusively, but it should be addressed with the whole class. By engaging them in a problem-solving process, she would demonstrate that Justin is an integral part of the class community. A future unit could encourage students to look at other ways inequity concerns come into play, perhaps by evaluating issues in their own communities.

- Although Ms. Thurston was mindful enough to call the park and inquire about accommodations, she took for granted that Justin would have a learning experience that paralleled that of his classmates when Ms. Parsons told her that accommodations were available. This reflects a sort of privilege that both Ms. Thurston and Ms. Parsons (as well as other people without mobility limitations) experience, but might not understand. Had Ms. Thurston asked for clarification about the available accommodations, she would not have been surprised upon arriving at the park. More importantly, she would have had an opportunity to make more equitable plans.

Case 8.3: Nut Allergy

- As the number of students being diagnosed with food allergies increases, educators should proactively enact policies that ensure student safety. For some students who, like Talia, have a nut allergy, even minimal exposure to nuts can mean a trip to the hospital. Talia's mother advocated for her safety because the extreme consequences that could occur if Talia accidentally was exposed to nuts was more important than others' desires to share an experience with their children. For adults who do not understand the potential severity of allergies, Ms. Thomas's request could have felt like an imposition. Mr. Hughes had taken many steps to protect Talia in the classroom, but he also might have benefited by helping educate other students' parents about the seriousness of Talia's allergies.

- When he attempted to address the growing tension in the classroom, Mr. Hughes noticed the conversation was causing Talia grief. He also noticed some students' comments reflected what was being communicated at home. Rather than causing additional tension by directly confronting what some students' parents were saying at home, Mr. Hughes could refocus the conversation on the classroom community and what equity looks like in that context. Whatever he chooses to do, it is important to take the spotlight off Talia and her mother.

- Although he might have wanted to validate the frustration felt by the parents who hoped to join the field trip but for whom there was no space, it was equally important that Mr. Hughes defended his commitment to advocating for Talia. In this sense, this case provides an opportunity to discuss the importance of staying committed to ideals of equity and justice even in the face of resistance.

Case 8.4: Behavior Management Missing the Mark

- Analyzing statistics pertaining to systemic inequity, and then creating action items based on that analysis, is important. However, action without preparation or training—without equity literacy—can result in unintentionally negative outcomes, such as resentment, confusion, and ineffective implementation. These outcomes become a cause of the student behaviors that staff were trying to prevent in the first place. Mr. Rhett needed support to address the issues but chose to use a strategy that was not working (the reward system) instead of seeking help. In addition to preparation and training, it is helpful to identify and utilize resources and expertise within the school. In this case, Mr. Paulson's strategies for connecting with students and engaging them effectively in class might be useful for his colleagues.

- While incentive systems can lead to positive changes for some students, there is danger in allocating time and resources to change student behavior if students are responding to inequitable or unwelcoming learning environments. We should make sure our equity strategies are solving our equity problems. Time and resources should be invested in fixing the environment, fixing the inequitable conditions in which Andre and Carson find themselves, not in fixing already marginalized students.

- Andre and Carson reported to Mr. Rhett the name calling and teasing they experienced at the school and mentioned that their teachers ignore it. By not addressing bias and bullying we send implicit messages to students who are or could be targets of inequity that we condone what they are experiencing. It is unjust to force students to endure this sort of situation, and then to punish them if they finally respond in kind.

Case 9.1: A New Club

- Gay-Straight Alliances and other student organizations built around particular affinity groups are designed to provide points of connection and systems of support for students who are marginalized in schools. So asking Lorraine, Jeff, Terrence, and Hu to start a Diversity Club defeats the purpose of the GSA. Also, the fact that the students are taking the lead on creating that space of safety for themselves can indicate that the school is not doing enough to create a safe, equitable atmosphere for them.
- Similarly, Ms. Livingsworth's solution is yet another indication of the school's troubling lack of urgency to ensure an equitable learning environment for LGBQ students (not to mention LGBQ staff, faculty, and other community members). By trying, in theory, to be "inclusive," the principal risks further alienating students who already might be feeling marginalized.
- Ms. Livingsworth's primary concern appears to be the possibility of alienating families she imagines to be in the majority: families who might be offended by a GSA. She could be right that some families would respond negatively to a GSA. On the other hand, some of those families might include LGBQ people. Certainly, if she allowed the students to start the GSA, Ms. Livingsworth

and her staff would have work to do explaining or defending it to some families. However, putting the comfort of privileged people ahead of equity for marginalized students guarantees the persistence of inequity.

Case 9.2: Date Auction

- It is important to consider how a Date Auction can conflict with the council's desire to help with the issue of youth homelessness. Many homeless youth struggle to find acceptance in schools, either because they are homeless or because of some dimension of their identities. LGBQ youth who are homeless often cite their families' rejection due to their sexual or gender identities as the cause of their homelessness. Additionally, homeless youth often are sexually exploited for money. A Date Auction and other sorts of heteronormative popularity contests trivialize the experiences faced by homeless youth and reinforce the destructive notion that some people are worthier than others of adulation.

- This scenario presents opportunities for many forms of inequity to manifest, including racism (and white privilege) and class inequality, in addition to sexism (and male privilege) and heterosexism (and heteronormativity). For example, although the school community is relatively affluent, this type of event is accessible only to students who can afford to participate; the event easily can turn into a display of who has more access to wealth. Additionally, bidding on someone's worth could be experienced by some members of the school community as a reminder of historical atrocities like the slave trade.

- Although Mr. Petrov has good intentions wanting students to take ownership of the project, his silence condones the students' idea, as well as the prejudiced and biased comments made by some of them. Although students in the case did not seem offended and even laughed at times, this does not necessarily reflect *agreement*. This case offers an opportunity to discuss how peer pressure can encourage complicity with inequity, even among people who are part of the groups being targeted.

- It might be easy to assume, because none of the students' sexual orientations were named explicitly in the case, that everybody at the council meeting identified as heterosexual. It is important to note this could be a faulty assumption.

Case 9.3: Outed at School

- This case provides an opportunity to discuss heteronormativity—the way heterosexuality is normalized in subtle and not-so-subtle ways. Examples might include how dances and other events are marketed, assumptions that all students have "mothers and fathers," conversations about dating, and discussions about literature and history in which people are presumed to be heterosexual even when no sexual orientation is specified.
- One reason Mr. Brooks was cautious about how he proceeded was that there might have been a student in his class who identified as LGBQ or who had an LGBQ relative. This possibility, or *probability*, is why it is important never to allow heterosexist language to go unnamed. Doing so can make all students feel the way it made Mr. Brooks feel when he was a student: that teachers condoned it.
- A common concern about introducing conversations about sexual orientation, homophobia, or heterosexism in schools is the perception that youth of certain ages are not old enough to talk about such matters. However, youth who use homophobic or heterosexist language already *are* talking about sexual orientation, and doing so in ways that are hurtful to their LGBQ peers or their peers who have LGBQ friends or family members. Children of any age can talk about these issues when provided effective facilitation.

Case 9.4: Two Moms

- Often, when somebody suggests children of a certain age are not old enough to talk about an injustice, they are thinking primarily of children from *privileged* identities. In this case, Denise is already beginning to experience bias from her peers. She likely has witnessed her mothers experiencing heterosexism, as well. If students are old enough to express or experience bias or injustice, they are old enough to talk about that bias or injustice.

- It might not always be possible to completely avoid conflict and controversy if we are committed to fostering an equitable and just classroom or school. Doing so requires us to respond to the kinds of situations to which Ms. Ribiero was responding in this case. One measure of a school's commitment to equity is its persistence to that commitment even in the face of controversy and complaints.
- Ms. Riberio made an important move by including a diverse collection of books in her classroom library. This would have been best practice even if Denise was not in her class. It's always better to be proactive rather than reactive when it pertains to diversity and social justice.

Case 10.1: Student Interpreter

- Although Marcella agreed to interpret for the conversation between her mother and Mr. Clark, teachers should ask parents' permission before requesting this sort of favor from students. Sometimes power dynamics arise in immigrant homes between parents and their children who might be more proficient in English. Asking children to interpret for adults could contribute to these negative dynamics.
- Mr. Clark intended to empower Marcella by praising her. The impact might not have been so positive. His praise for her ability to speak two languages might have made her mother feel embarrassed since she was not yet proficient in English.
- Rather than using a student to discuss a student issue with a parent, Mr. Clark might have asked a bilingual staff member to interpret. Alternatively, he could have had Maria explain to her mother that Mr. Clark would be calling her to arrange a time to meet with him and an interpreter. It's important for Maria to take ownership of the conversation and for Ms. Montes to not feel self-conscious of her language abilities.

Case 10.2: English-Only

- Research has shown for decades that English-only policies are harmful to the morale *and the learning* of students who are learning English. These policies also contribute to the alienation of their parents and families. Given these realities, it is important to consider that these policies often are ideological responses, reactive in nature, and not based on evidence of best teaching practices.

- Ms. Mancini and Ms. de Leon are in a difficult situation. There are times in all educators' careers when we must make decisions about the extent to which we will implement policies and practices we believe are harmful to students or colleagues. Ms. Mancini and Ms. de Leon will need to be mindful of the implications of their decisions about how to proceed.

- Students who are learning English can feel exhausted by the end of the day because of how hard they are concentrating on language while also focusing on other aspects of school. Being able to speak in their home languages for brief periods throughout the day provides relief so they are better able to focus. This reality might be difficult to understand for people who have not experienced submersion in an environment in which a language other than their home language is spoken. One way to cultivate this sort of empathy is having teachers sit through a sample lesson or staff development that is conducted entirely in a language with which they are not familiar. Although these experiences do not recreate the full magnitude of discomfort students who are learning English might experience in an English-only environment, they offer short, sometimes powerful, glimpses into that experience.

- Despite popular perception, contemporary immigrants who arrive to the U.S. not speaking English are learning English more quickly than any previous generation of immigrants. It is important to challenge the stereotype that immigrants do not want to learn English or do not want their children to learn English. It also is important to remind ourselves that many people whose families have been in the U.S. for multiple generations, including white people, have ancestors who were discriminated against due to *their* inability to speak English.

Case 10.3: Family Night

- The teachers designed the event based on their perceptions of what would make an ideal family night. They assumed all parents would arrive at the start time, sit quietly, listen, then go home. One thing they did not consider was the importance in many cultures of social interaction, communication, and connection. The importance placed upon these dynamics does not reflect disinterest in school or in an event's official program. The social interaction that occurred was a positive, though unintentional, outcome.

- The teachers were thoughtful in translating the flier for Family Night. However, they did not think to provide interpretation for the evening's program or translation for the handout. Given this reality, it could be that the ELL families were discussing the presentation and helping to interpret it for one another, standing in the back to avoid disrupting other attendees. Alternatively, families might not have asked questions if the handout was self-explanatory or if they felt it would be a burden to the teachers to stay and answer questions after the event ended.

- The event produced high turnout from families who do not typically attend functions at Crestwood. This is an accomplishment that cannot be quantified. Instead of feeling discouraged, Mr. Nelson and the other teachers might focus on finding ways to build on this accomplishment.

Case 10.4: A New Task Force

- When planning to solicit parent input and improve attendance at decision-making meetings, it is important to consider the school's *history* of outreach. Have under-represented families felt welcome? Might they be fearful of negative repercussions if they are critical of the school?

- This case provides an opportunity to explore barriers that might inhibit some parents from participating in school activities, such as financial constraints that limit access to childcare or transportation or work schedules for people who work multiple jobs or don't have paid leave. Language barriers also could limit participation, even if translated documents are sent home. Even if interpreters are available, families might feel their opinions aren't valued. We should train ourselves to consider these possibilities rather than defaulting to a presumption that a lack of on-site family involvement reflects a lack of concern about education.

- There is danger in assuming one, or even several, voices from certain demographic groups represent the rest of the group. Though Ms. Ahmed had good rapport with families and felt she was an advocate, other task force members should not ask her to speak on behalf of other people, just as they should not assume Mr. Webb will speak on behalf of all parents.

Case 11.1: An Assigned Nickname

- Given the power dynamics between teachers and students, sometimes a choice really isn't a choice. Sarai might have agreed to the nickname out of respect for Ms. Goodwin or out of a desire to avoid the uncomfortable situation of having to "correct" Ms. Goodwin's pronunciation of her name. In either case, it's important to understand the situations in which we place students. Sarai might not express a desire to go by her given name if she wants to please her teacher.
- Some parents feel they should not challenge their children's teachers. Sarai's mother nodded in agreement with Sarai's nickname but might not be comfortable with the decision, or might be afraid of ramifications if she disappoints the teacher, which could explain her change in disposition during the conference.
- Names are important. In many cases they tie students to ancestors or to the places from where our ancestors hailed, and these ties can be particularly strong for immigrants or first-generation U.S. citizens. Changing a child's name in school, or even giving them a nickname, can impact their entire school career. It's important to learn how parents pronounce their children's names. That will be your guide for how you should pronounce them. Students might not feel comfortable correcting you.

Case 11.2: I'm Not Black

- Rather than assigning Abiola a mentor based on her own criteria for who would be best, Ms. Lee could have asked for a volunteer. She also could have asked Abiola whether he wanted a mentor. Certainly, though, she should have been more careful not to turn her mentor program into a social experiment by presuming she could help create a bridge between the African American and Nigerian students by matching Warren with Abiola. Additionally, we should allow students to self-identify instead of grouping them based on our perceptions.

- The trouble with color-blindness is that it masks, not just difference, but the ramifications of difference. When we are determined not to see difference it can become all too easy also not to see inequities or biases that are associated with difference. Students' racial and ethnic (and other) identities influence the ways they experience school, largely because people's assumptions and expectations of them are informed by those racial and ethnic (and other) identities. As long as racism exists, color-blindness merely masks this reality, blocking us from seeing and addressing its roots and trivializing the experiences of people of color.

- In many if not *most* cases in which new waves of immigrants have entered the U.S., those immigrants have experienced tremendous amounts of injustice. This is even true, for example, for waves of Irish and Italian immigrants, who once experienced bigotry similar to what Mexican and Central American immigrants experience today. This case provides an opportunity to reflect on why this pattern persists. Consider what makes people whose own ancestors immigrated to the U.S., perhaps facing bigotry in the process, turn around and aim their bigotry at today's immigrants.

Case 11.3: A Legacy of Privilege on the Soccer Pitch

- This case provides an opportunity to discuss how national policy concerns are often debated on the backs of youth. This is especially true of immigration and language policies. In this case, all the players trying out for the team are impacted if they are hearing the sentiments of the adults in their homes and communities. Mr. Rosenthal should be mindful of this when he communicates expectations for the tryouts.

- Sometimes, when people support their positions on issues by referring to a "legacy" or "tradition," they are subtly demonstrating a sense of entitlement or a fear of change. In this case, the desire to have the team remain "homegrown" reflects this entitlement or fear. Many educational inequities and biases remain in schools in the name of "tradition," such as through the continued use of stereotype-inspired American Indian athletic team mascots or school names.

- Mr. Rosenthal is right to feel the expectations given to him are unjust, especially since they are in response to a threat from a group of parents. Not only does going along with the expectation convey the message that the parents' behavior is acceptable, it also sets a precedent for the soccer program, and perhaps for other programs, in future years.

Case 11.4: Family Involvement

- Although Mr. Rolnick provided various opportunities for parents to volunteer, many could be interpreted as simple tasks meant to assist teachers rather than meaningful ways to engage students. Although some parents might enjoy filing books or making copies, others might prefer being involved more directly by tutoring, reading aloud, or assisting with other learning activities in the classroom or with their own children at home.

- Mr. Rolnick equated volunteering with family involvement, but these are different in nature. Parent involvement can take many forms, including simply asking children about their school day, encouraging them to read or do homework, or following up on a phone call from the teacher. Joel's parents were involved, as they attended conferences and offered to address concerns at home. We should avoid mistaking their hesitance to volunteer at the school as a lack of concern for Joel's education.

- One barrier to family involvement that receives too little attention is some parents' own negative experiences with school. An experience some people take for granted, such as walking into an elementary school for a meeting and feeling welcome, is not a universal experience. For people who felt alienated as students, walking into the building can feel like entering an unwelcoming cultural or political space. It can be uncomfortable; it might even feel hostile. Some parents might still see in schools the inequities and biases they experienced as students and thus choose to involve themselves in their children's education without coming to the school. This reality can be particularly difficult to see for those of us who always felt validated at school.

Case 11.5: My Uncle

- In some cultures, all elders, or at least close family friends who are elders, are referred to as "Uncle" or "Aunt" as a sign of respect. Abdi's uncle might have been unrelated by blood, but still a trusted friend who was invited to attend the meeting in place of his father. Because Ms. Klein and Ms. Larson's cultural views only recognized terms like "Uncle" as referring to family members, they assumed Abdi's family, and others in the school who acted similarly, were deceitful. This assumption can have a harmful impact on relationships between teachers and students as well as students' families.
- Ms. Klein assumed her concerns would not be communicated to Abdi's father. She felt frustrated assuming Abdi's behavior would not change because his father did not attend the conference. Unfortunately, she discredited Abdi's mother's authority based only on her observations from Family Night. A more constructive, more effective, way for her to view the situation would have been to realize that Abdi's mother was *very much* engaged in addressing his behavior concerns. This was evident because she addressed his behavior at Family Night and attended the conference with an additional influential person in Abdi's life.

- Students whose home lives are blends of multiple cultures can feel conflicted between the norms of those cultures. A student who feels embarrassed because of some aspect of her identity, especially when teachers respond negatively to it, might respond by disengaging. Alternatively, the student's desire to be accepted by the school community might cause a change in behavior that can conflict with traditions in the house, causing conflict within the family. It is important that we as educators learn not to exacerbate these tensions.

References

Bonney, K. M. (2015). Case study teaching method improves student performance and perceptions of learning gains. *Journal of Microbiology and Biology Education, 16*(1), 21–28.

Brown, K. D., & Kraehe, A. M. (2010). The complexities of teaching the complex: Examining how future educators construct understandings of sociocultural knowledge and schooling. *Educational Studies, 46,* 91–115.

Darling-Hammond, L. (2006). *Powerful Teacher Education: Lessons from Exemplary Programs.* San Francisco, CA: Jossey-Bass.

Foster, R. H., McBeth, M. K., & Clemons, R. S. (2010). Public policy pedagogy: Mixing methodologies using case studies. *Journal of Public Affairs Education, 16*(4), 517–540.

Gallego, A., Fortunato, M. S., Rossi, S. L., Korol, S. E., & Moretton, J. A. (2013). Case method in the teaching of food safety. *Journal of Food Science Education, 12*(3), 42–47.

Gallucci, K. (2006). Learning concepts with cases. *Journal of College Science Teaching, 36*(2), 16–20.

Gorski, P. C. (2016). Equity literacy: More than celebrating diversity. *Diversity in Education, 11*(1), 12–15.

Gorski, P. C. (2017). Rethinking the role of "culture" in educational equity: From cultural competence to equity literacy. *Multicultural Perspectives, 18*(4), 221–226.

Gorski, P. C., & Swalwell, K. (2015). Equity literacy for all. *Educational Leadership, 72*(6), 34–40.

Leonard, E. C., & Cook, R. A. (2010). Teaching with cases. *Journal of Teaching in Travel & Tourism, 10,* 95–101.

Mills, J., West, C., Langtree, T., Usher, K., Henry, R., Chamberlain-Salaun, J., & Mason, M. (2014). "Putting it together": Unfolding case studies and high-fidelity simulation in the first-year of an undergraduate nursing curriculum. *Nurse Education in Practice, 14*(1), 12–17.

Naumes, W., & Naumes, M. (1999). *The Art and Craft of Case Writing*. Thousand Oaks, CA: Sage.

Nieto, S., & Bode, P. (2011). *Affirming Diversity: The Sociopolitical Context of Multicultural Education*. Boston, MA: Pearson.

Rosenbaum, R. S., Gilboa, A., & Moscovitch, M. (2014). Case studies continue to illuminate the cognitive neuroscience of memory. *Annals of the New York Academy of Sciences, 1316*, 105–133.

Swalwell, K. (2011). Why our students need "equity literacy." *Teaching Tolerance Blog*, www.tolerance.org/blog/why-our-students-need-equity-literacy, accessed January 13, 2013.